Find more of my work at my blog:

www.theauthorstack.com

Find all my work at my website:

www.russellnohelty.com

Bookbub:

https://www.bookbub.com/profile/russell-nohelty

ADVANCED GROWTH TACTICS FOR AUTHORS

By:
Russell Nohelty

Edited by:
Lily Luchesi

Proofread by:
Toni Cox

INTRODUCTION

This is not a book. It might resemble a book and be bound like a book, but a book has a beginning, middle, and end.

It posits a thesis statement and then produces evidence to support that thesis statement. By the end of a book, you should be changed from the person you were and transformed into a new type of person.

At the very least, you should leave a book with the tools necessary to accomplish a task.

This collection of words does none of that. It is simply that…a collection of words. They were written to either my email list or on social media between August 2015 and December 2022.

They exist in this form because these musings were well-received enough that I didn't want to discard them, but they do not fit neatly into any project I am working on, either by myself or with my Writer MBA business partner, Monica Leonelle.

I write a lot about Kickstarter, direct sales, and retailer sales for our work together, but I also write a lot about other things related to a writerly life, and these are those posts.

I don't expect you to care about this, except that many people do very much care about these musings. They tell me how much they like them often and how much they wish these writings were compiled in a place they could reference.

As a person who never likes to let good work evaporate into the ether, I kept them together. I have submitted them to several blogs and asked Monica if there was anything we could do with them, but like I said before, they just didn't fit anywhere.

That does not mean they are without value. So, I kept them, gathering them like a little dragon, figuring that, at some point, they would be relevant.

Eventually, I started to compile them, expecting to have a few thousand words. I was surprised that I had written tens of thousands of words and that it was enough to bind them all into a book-type object.

But this is not a book.

It is a collection of words that struggle to encapsulate what it means to be a writer. I do not always talk about it well, and these are not all pleasant.

However, I stand by them all. They are my words, after all, so I better stand behind them. I think many of them are good. Some of them might move you. Others might make you angry.

Either reaction is okay. I am still surprised anything I say has any value, and I appreciate the heck out of those who find value in them.

Maybe that's you, and that is fab. Maybe you will find no value in them, and that's less fab but perfectly fine, too.

If you read this expecting any sort of order, you will be disappointed because this is not a book. I honestly can't emphasize that enough.

I hope you enjoy it all the same, though.

-Russell

PLANNING SEASON

How does my process work?

When I start planning, I usually ask myself, *"how can I do ten years of growth in one year?"*

Unfortunately, I've gotten to the point where a lot of that growth is dependent on OTHER people, which is frustrating, but you can only control what you can control.

This is the question that got me from nothing to where I am now, but it becomes harder to do over the long term as the levels become harder to navigate and jump between. I find myself now worrying as much about the fall as the climb.

Now, however, I know what a good year looks like for me, and I can plan around that, at least.

While I'm figuring these big questions out, I'm mapping out what worked and what didn't in the last year, along with what brought me bliss and what I turned away from.

It's awesome to cut those things out that no longer serve me, and it's liberating to be freed of that burden once I pull the trigger.

This will usually take me until December to figure out, but I start around now to give my brain enough time to think.

I want to give myself time to think through every implication before I cut something out or double down on it.

Once I figure out the general "narrative" of the year, I cut everything that's not working to get my schedule as LEAN as possible so I can build back up from there.

Then, drop-in any events for 2021 I committed to in RED and any that I plan to attend in YELLOW.

This includes fulfillment days when I will be packing Kickstarters and other orders. Book delivery is nebulous, but you can usually peg it to a couple of weeks' window and then be flexible from there.

Usually, my show schedule is full, but for 2021 it will only be virtual conventions and potential shows later in the year.

Then, I take any planned projects (get a new logo, website redesign, courses, masterminds, etc.) that aren't money-makers and place them into my workflow. There are money-LOSERS in the short term but huge money-makers over time.

Finally, I drop in any planned promotions outside of launches.

I try to make my schedule look like a wave, with four different peaks and then four valleys, where I'm going from launch to promotion and back again.

The rest of the days are GREEN, which means a writing day, where my schedule is as follows: get up at 6 am, write from 9-2 pm, go on a walk/nap/read until 4 pm, and then meetings or admin work from 4-6 pm.

Unless absolutely necessary, I try not to plan anything during weekdays before 2 pm. I do pretty well already scheduling meetings from 4-6 pm only, but 2 pm is my absolute earliest availability.

By then, my calendar is pretty full, and I start getting to work planning the budget for everything, the expected return for each project, and try to balance my expected cash flow accordingly.

I know this may seem anal to many people, but it works for me to visualize my calendar, my promotions, and my cash flow and ensure I don't get overleveraged.

In fact, my goal is to be MASSIVELY underleveraged because I know there will be lots of projects that come up during the year which I want to leap on, and being underleveraged gives me the ability to jump on them when they come up, and gives me elasticity in the rigidity of my schedule.

Every year I've cut more and more things, which has given me more and more elasticity to do more and more interesting projects.

PLANNING YOUR BOOKISH YEAR

I've talked about planning before, but it's fresh on my mind right now, so I wanted to revisit the three steps I use to plan every year and how you can have your most bookish year ever.

1. CORE RELEASE SCHEDULE

The most important part to get right is your core book release schedule.

Honestly, I like having my schedule planned a year ahead of time. In fact, I've already finished production on 9 out of my 10 scheduled books for next year, and good publishing companies have their books planned at least 18 months in advance.

I'm already deep into production on 2022 books, having completed writing my first book for my January 2022 release, and am over 40,000 words into writing the second one, out of four, which will release then.

Being a year ahead means I never have to freak out about something going wrong. I know it's not something everyone can do, but I do not do well with panic, and the only way I can survive as a writer is by being far ahead of my schedule.

It started as a necessity when making comics, as I had to build up a buffer with my artist to release anything, but over the years, I've found it lovely to have everything planned and ready months in advance.

It also makes promotion WAY easier, allowing me to set the pace for the following year without worrying about catching up to meet a rapidly approaching deadline.

It even allows me to slot new books into my calendar as time permits. My launch for *How NOT to Invade Earth* in November was a fortuitous happenstance that came about because I had time to plan and capitalize on an opportunity.

Seasons greeting

I try to think of my release calendar in seasons, with every launch being the crescendo of the wave I'm building up to or recovering from. Knowing that, I set my launches based on when I know I can crescendo effectively.

There are three parts to a launch - Prep, Launch, and Recovery. In prep, I build up to my next launch. Then, there is the launch itself. Finally, in recovery, I give both myself and my fans a chance to relax and catch their breath before we do it again.

For me, that means January, March, June, and September, I launch books. I have always had effective launches in those months for different reasons.

In January and June, there are fewer books launching, so I can capitalize on that with my less popular books. In March and September, there are tons of books launching, so I put out my most popular books then so they get the most eyeballs on them.

Once that is set, I know I need to spend a month building up to that launch, which means the lowest point on the release wave will occur every year in December, February, May, and August.

It looks like this when I break it down.

- **January** - Prep (01/01-01/04), Launch (01/05-01/21)
- **February** - Recover (01/22-02/09), Prep (02/10-02/28)
- **March** - Prep (03/01-03/15), Launch (03/15-03/31)
- **April** - Launch (04/01-04/14), Recover (04/15-04/30)
- **May** - Recover (05/01-05/14) -Prep (05/15-05/31)
- **June** - Prep (06/01-06/14) Launch (06/15-06/30)
- **July** - Launch (07/01) Recover (07/02-07/31)
- **August** - Recover (08/01-08/05), Prep (08/06-08/31)
- **September** - Prep (09/01-09/06) Launch (09/07-09/31)
- **October** - Launch (10/01-10/07) Recover (10/08-10/31)
- **November** - Recover (11/01-11/30)
- **December** - Recover (12/01-12/03), Prep (12/04-12/31)

My biggest book launches last 31 days, and my shortest can be as short as five days. It all depends on the project and how much I think people can stand me talking about it.

It's important to note that this is my launch schedule for core books ONLY. I lay this out FIRST, before anything else, including experimental projects and other things I'm adding to the mix.

Then, I plan every other launch around this schedule, as it is my moneymaker. It took me a LONG time to learn this, and it wasn't until I did that I had any consistency in my career.

Once I have planned these core launches, I figure out what else I want to try in the remaining time.

This brings us to the next thing.

2. NEW PROJECTS TO TRY

Every year, businesses shed dead weight from projects that aren't working and add new things for the following year.

Sometimes, it's a wild idea that comes out of thin air like a shot in the dark.

These new projects are CRITICAL to the long-term success of your business, whether they are a new series (I am launching one next year), a new format (audio, mobile game, podcast), or an entirely new line of business (merch, subscription).

This is how you diversify and grow, but it is absolutely CRITICAL that these do not interrupt your company's core business, which is why you need to get your book launches in first.

They are how you pay the bills and what your existing fans expect, and they take priority. If you aren't making money from your books now, then they are HOW you want to make your money, so they still need to be first on your list of priorities because you will train your readers when to expect new books from you.

Only after you lay down these launches can you see gaps in your schedule for new projects.

Those are my ONLY windows for NEW projects and forms of business. Otherwise, I am interrupting core business and my money-makers. I made this mistake for MANY years, and it is always a mistake.

You deal with your money-makers FIRST, and then work your new ideas AROUND those launches.

Last year, for instance, I knew that March, September, and January were good times to launch, so I put my biggest-selling products (*Cthulhu is Hard to Spell,* The Godsverse Chronicles, and *Ichabod Jones: Monster Hunter)* into those spots.

Last year I had a significant gap in June, and I put a "trial" product, a bunch of stand-alone novels, into that spot. It worked, adding almost $10,000 to my bottom line, and this year I am launching a new series into that spot, trying to firm it up as a consistent moneymaker for me.

I also had nothing planned in August, and I launched a free book offer that month, adding $2,000+ to my bottom line. Both of those were successful tests, but neither interfered with my core business.

They don't always work out successfully, though. In 2019, I had nothing for November, so I launched my new podcast in that gap. It did NOT work as planned, but at least it didn't affect my other launches.

New product launches won't always be perfect, but they don't have to be. You are testing to expand your business…which is why they can't interfere with your core book launches. You need to consider those book launches immovable and sacred and then plan around them.

How do you have time for all these new projects when your schedule is already filled?

Well, that brings us to the final step.

3. CUTTING DOWN

Now, if you're anything like me a couple of years ago, you have no time in your schedule for new things because your days are filled to the brim ostly with garbage.

The only way to fix this is to cut things that don't work to make room in your schedule.

There's a good case to be made for doing this BEFORE you add things, but I like to do it after because I need to know why I'm giving up something else and that I'm doing it to make room for something significantly better or at least more exciting.

The more I visualize what I'm adding, the more ruthless I can be with cutting things out that don't service me.

Last year, I added a podcast back into my schedule, and this year I decided to do 100 podcast guest appearances to see if they serviced me. Neither did, and I had to cut them moving forward to make room for what does work, namely, writing more books and launching more products to my readers.

However, it didn't affect my schedule because I had huge gaps for this kind of testing written into my calendar. Your goal is to be VASTLY underleveraged time-wise, so you can try new things and see if they work.

Sometimes, the things you take on means taking on new projects, like the three virtual conferences I ran in 2020 or starting up a book marketing business…but that also means you have to be ruthless with knowing what doesn't work, so you can cut it like I did with almost all my appearances from 2020, my podcast, and most of my conference chairmanships.

It's only because I had the time that I could take time for those things, and only because I know how valuable that time is to me that I could cut back when they didn't service me.

Just like your publishing schedule, you need to take on things like the tide coming in and let them go like the tide going out. You'll never know if something works until you try it, no matter how many books you read. However, just because you try something doesn't mean you need to keep doing it.

Even if you don't do other things like teaching or consulting, you might take on new book series like the tide, trying new genres or conventions to see if they work, but you need to be able to jettison new series just as easily. You cannot get caught up in a series that's not working, especially if it's taking time away from series that might work.

When you are just getting started, you have NO IDEA what will work, so you're going to be doing a lot of crazy things, doing a bunch of different launches, and trying many things.

However, when one thing works, you lock it in. Over time you'll be able to say, "okay, I launch this book series in January, and this other one in November, and when I launch in May, it doesn't go well", because you'll have tried it all.

It's trial and error at first until you have your process.

I know writers who launch every two weeks and ones that launch once a year. It's whatever works for you, but you have to know what works, what new things you want to try, and what you're willing to cut so that every year you get more precise and deadly with your publishing slate, stacking things that work on top of each other.

That's what it's all about, really.

The reason why people who have a bunch of books sell more is that they have found what works, and they've done it enough that they can stack things that work amazingly on top of each other until every launch and every project is effective.

REALISTIC ADVICE

Just because somebody offers you realistic advice doesn't mean they are being negative. People that blow smoke up your butt about how you can accomplish anything are not doing you any favors.

Anything worth doing is hard.

Saying something like, "you'll probably have to put out at least ten and likely more like twenty books before you have a legit shot to make a living as a writer," and, "if you don't write in very specific categories like romance or thriller while writing to market and releasing often, it's going to be really hard for you, and you'll have to put out even more books," aren't negative statements.

They are statements of facts. If knowing the facts prevents you from doing something, maybe you shouldn't do it.

Yes, some people make it without doing those things, but they are uncommon. Usually, people that hit the market quickly have hit on an upcoming trend or underserved niche.

Additionally, telling somebody that to make a living in comics, they will need to become comfortable with selling at shows and launching Kickstarters and that there is no real way around it isn't a negative comment.

It's a statement of fact. It is nearly impossible to make a living in comics without using one or both mediums, at least for independent creators.

Foregoing those two avenues drastically undercuts your ability to survive in the comics game, especially if you also eschew Patreon.

You have two options with those statements, refuse them, and then five years later, say, "WHY DIDN'T ANYBODY TELL ME THESE THINGS?" which I literally hear every day.

Or you can understand the limitations and either lean into them or, with eyes open, buck those trends and make your own way.

None of that is negative. It's realistic from somebody who has been there before and is trying to paint a picture.

Yes, some people will use those facts to turn around and say, "so you shouldn't even try" or "just give up," which is negative, but unflattering statements of fact are not negative on their own.

Facts are neither negative nor positive. They are facts, and if you willfully ignore them or think somebody is trying to hold you back by relaying them to you, you're going to smack headfirst into them.

GUILT CAN'T SCALE

I had a conversation with a creator recently. What we talked about gnawed away at me all weekend. It's something I hear all the time. It impedes so many creatives from moving to the next level.

He was bitter because nobody he knew wanted to buy his book.

He went to them hat in hand and couldn't get anybody to take a chance on what he had to offer. He didn't understand why his family would forsake him while they bought whatever celebrities told them to buy.

"It's not personal," I told him.

"But why?" he asked me. "They are my family. They should be supporting me more than some celebrity."

I only had one reply. "Guilt can't scale."

You can't guilt people into buying something. It makes them bitter and resentful. They see your panhandling as an obligation they want to get rid of as soon as possible. They won't become long-term customers. Even if you somehow get their money, all you've done is make yourself a nuisance. You haven't made a customer for life.

Make no mistake, that's what you are after in the end. One of the biggest predictors of overall success is customer lifetime value. Obligation does not build a happy customer and is never appreciated. Think about the things you are obligated to do. You are obligated to pay your mortgage. You are obligated to do chores. You are obligated to take your dog to the vet.

All those things suck.

Nobody willingly takes on an obligation with a smile. You can only force an obligation on somebody. And you don't want to force anybody into buying your product. You want them to buy it happily. You want them to buy all your products because it fits a need in their life, even if that need is just edifying their soul.

Let me give you some statistics. I've run three Kickstarter campaigns in the last year. The first one for *Katrina Hates the Dead* raised $8,500 from 294 backers. The second one for *My Father Didn't Kill Himself* raised $3,300 from 155 backers. The third for *I Can't Stop Tooting: A Love Story* raised $2,100 from 65 backers.

Now, I have over 20,000 twitter followers, 2,000 Facebook friends, and 7,000 Instagram followers, on top of 2,000 people on my mailing list. That's a reach of around 30,000 people. And yet I only had a total of 500 people back those projects combined. That's a little under 2% of my reach that decided to buy from me.

I could be mad about that. I could sulk. I could cry. I could pound my fist in the air. I could yell at the people who didn't back.

But what will that get me?

It won't get more people to back my projects. It won't make me more money. All it will do is ruin friendships and destroy family ties. On top of all that, it would make me an angry, spiteful, vindictive man. That's no way to go through life.

So I left the 98% alone and focused my products on the 2%. Those are the people who like my sense of humor. They are the ones who resonate with my message. Those people want to buy my products. They have the highest customer lifetime value. They are my target audience. That's no different than every other company. This is how all companies succeed. They focus their message on the 2% of the marketplace that resonates with their message.

If I know 2% of people will back my projects, I can develop a plan to find more people like my ideal market. It's incumbent on me to cast the biggest net so that 2% is as big as humanly possible. If I have 3,000,000 people in that net, the 2% that buy will get me exponentially more revenue than the 30,000 I have right now.

There are multiple ways to increase your profit, but focusing your attention on who isn't buying from you isn't one of them.

You don't want people to buy things out of obligation or guilt anyway. You want them to buy because they WANT to buy. Those are the people who are in your ideal market. Those are the people you can build a business around. You will never convince somebody your product is cool if they don't see a need for it.

Maybe, along the way, you'll guilt a couple of people into buying from you. But those people are short-term gain. They aren't going to buy every one of your products. They aren't in for the long haul. They aren't going to support your entire career.

You will do well to remember that and become okay with it. In the short term, it hurts when your family doesn't buy from you, especially when you are just getting started. In the beginning, you are clawing for every dollar, but that's why strategic planning is so important. That's why you can't focus on the short term. You have to focus on the long term.

And in the long term, understanding that it's not personal is one of the most important skills you can learn for your business and your sanity. After all, guilt can't scale.

MAKING A LIVING

If you want to have the best chance of being a successful author, then you should write one of the following genres:

1. **Romance** (including reverse harem, erotica, paranormal, et al.)
2. **Thriller** (including crime, mystery, and supernatural suspense)
3. **Cozy** mystery/paranormal cozy
4. **Military sci-fi/space opera**

These genres have the largest group of readers to pull from, and they are always hungry for new books, like a read-a-book-a-day-type of hungry.

Depending on the genre, there are tropes that people expect from each of those books, and you should follow each of them. Generally, this is a list of 5-6 things that every book will have.

For instance, in romance, there will almost always be a meet-cute, a misunderstanding, and a grand gesture. In mystery, there will always be a crime, a false accusation, and a final reveal.

Then, there is a convention for each genre's covers and blurbs that will give them the best chance of success. For cozy mysteries, putting baked goods or cats on the cover will help them sell. For sexy times romance, a man-chest on the cover helps them sell.

Follow all of those conventions, then write at least three books in a series, and hopefully more like 4-5, and you have the best chance for success. Again, a series with every genre and subgenre is different.

For some subset of the writing population, maybe even the majority that love those genres and are fine writing for tropey books, you're going to do just fine.

If you don't want to do that, though, if you want to write in a different genre or don't want to write in a series, well, that's fine, but things are going to be MUCH HARDER for you.

AND the conventions people talk about for marketing and sales WON'T WORK FOR YOU, at least not nearly as well as writing in one of those genres above.

Are there ways to sell in niche genres (which I count as anything NOT listed above)? Absolutely. It's harder, but it's doable. I write in mythological fantasy and comics, two niches of niches, and I still made a decent living last year, but absolutely NOBODY would be able to guess it from my Amazon page or my reviews.

You aren't going to get there in one book or ten books if you write in those off-genres.

...but, Russell, Schlomo Jordan writes 17th-century horror about monkey pirates, and he makes a great living.

Yes, some people will defy the odds.

Plenty of people write in historical fiction or epic fantasy that break through, but it's much harder, and there isn't a set path.

There are things off-genre authors do to stand out. In fantasy, the two that usually rise to the top are dragons and fairy tales. If you can incorporate one of those two things into your fantasy stories, you improve your odds of standing out.

Most successful authors right now are in one of the above four categories. Notice I didn't even list straight fantasy (though it is represented in paranormal romance, paranormal cozy, and supernatural suspense) or other types of sci-fi besides military space opera.

It's not likely you'll break out and be a huge hit in ANY of those other genres.

Can it happen? Yeah.

Will it probably look weird compared to your author friends? Very much, yeah.

Will it likely take forever? Oh yeah, that's a ten-four.

This isn't to discourage you.

But you should know that NOW before you get started because that woman who writes three contemporary romances and makes $4k a month that just blew past you on their first release?

They are writing on genre with the conventional tropes, cover, and blurb for that genre, slotting themselves into a great position to succeed early.

It's not easy, but it's far easier than writing off-genre. Niche genre books need a whole lot more planning and thought because the landing zone is much narrower and the upside much smaller.

And you should know that going in. Write whatever thing you want, in any genre you want, but if you want to succeed off the bat, then you should write in the top four genres.

If you don't, then stop comparing yourself to people who do. Success will look a lot different for you than for them.

CHASE THE JOY

Historically, I have not been a happy person. I suffer from both anxiety and depression. I am relentlessly negative as well. However, early in 2018, I set out to change that as much as I could. I decided my motto for 2018 was "chase the joy".

I knew I wanted to stop doing things I hated and start doing things I loved.

I didn't even know I could be happy at the beginning of the year. Everything I did was filled with misery. However, soon enough, I found that interlaced with my misery were moments where the dopamine hit me.

It was only for a moment at first, but like a ping in a great ocean, I used it as a guide. Every time I felt that dopamine hit, I would try to analyze why I was so happy in that one brief moment.

Over time, I was able to put together a list of things that made me happy, and even though I was still mostly miserable, I started to chase those moments.

It started with my personal life, but it soon seeped over to my work, and I found the things that I really loved doing, the shows that resonated with me, and the parts of my job that I enjoyed...and I tried to do them as much as possible.

I assumed my revenue would go down as I cut out the miserable tasks I hated, but I made more money this year than I did last year.

And I did it in ways that mostly brought me joy.

Not all ways, of course. Honestly, there are still a lot of days that suck butt. There are things in business you need to do which just aren't fun. There are moments, even in the fun part, that are miserable.

However, for the most part, I could stretch those moments of joy into whole hours or even days. For me, that's a huge accomplishment.

And it all started with a simple three-word motto.

"Chase the joy."

10 THINGS I KNOW

1. **Bad luck can tank a career.** I have seen it happen many times. They were in the wrong place, at the wrong time, and the universe screwed them unfairly. It's heartbreaking every time.
2. **Good things happen to bad people, and bad things happen to good people.** The reverse is also true, even if you don't see it.
3. **If you have enough projects going, eventually, good luck and hard work can save a career.** I have also seen this happen, often with the exact same people who lost their careers to bad luck. Every project has its own luck baked into it, and every project is a chance to turn it all around. Once you do, everything else you've made has more value.
4. **You have absolutely no idea which project will pop off or where.** The book that has made me the most getting optioned is one most of my fans have never read and never heard of (*My Father Didn't Kill Himself,* FWIW). Ichabod and The Godsverse Chronicles, my two most successful and enduring works, have made $0 in Hollywood during that time.
5. **The only thing you truly control is the work you do.** You can give yourself better odds by understanding marketing, sales, writing to market, and all that stuff, but even then, you can't control who resonates with

your book. You can show it to them. You can tell them about it. You cannot force them to buy it, read it, or love it. The only thing you truly control is the work. If you don't love the work, you should stop doing it because even when you have a career doing this, all you have to look forward to is more work.

6. **For some people, the path is clear from the beginning.** For almost everyone, though, it takes searching through the mire and the muck, sometimes forever.

7. **If you believe in something enough, double down on it.** However, if you're not ready to be proven a fool, or push a boulder up a hill for a long time until people see things your way, then pivot to something else. There are infinite projects, and they all have within them the chance to break through and completely change your career.

8. **Making money doesn't determine the importance of something.** Some of my favorite things I've ever made are also my worst sellers.

9. **There is no shame in doing things for the money. We all have to eat.** There is also no shame in doing something for the passion, even if it never makes a dime.

10. **Just because a project fails now doesn't mean it's a failure.** It took seven years for Ichabod to find an audience, and many of my best works never found theirs. They were still worth doing, though.

BONUS

11. **If all else fails, you are not a failure.** This is the most important one of all.

"THIS IS A BAD IDEA."

A couple of years ago, when I was going hard at The Complete Creative and looking to relaunch my podcast, I messaged a friend about being a guest, and she said (and I'm paraphrasing here):

"I think this is a bad idea."

I was taken aback, so I asked why.

"You're doing too much," she replied. "Why don't you try to be a writer for a while?"

It didn't make much sense then, and I disregarded it immediately. However, over the next year, especially as we went through COVID and I was frantically trying to keep from losing everything, her words kept nagging at me.

I was spending a lot of time doing things I didn't want to do just so I could make enough money to do the things I wanted to do, like writing.

I was doing dozens of podcasts a week, book marketing, killing myself to scrape by, and the whole time I wasn't writing ANYTHING.

While we were in COVID lockdown, I told my wife I had no time to write because, again, I was trying to do everything, especially at the beginning of COVID, making me super stressed.

She then said, "It seems like you're just doing all this other stuff so you can funnel all your money into writing. What if you didn't do that other stuff?"

She was right, too, as was my friend.

I would be spending five hours on podcasts for coaching and courses, and then take whatever money I earned and funnel it all into books and such, which meant I was spending 10 hours only to do five hours of work I cared about and was actually moving the career I wanted forward.

I didn't care about owning a course business or building a membership community. I was just doing it because people said it was a good way to make money that could then be funneled into writing.

After thinking about it and trying to come up with a plan for months, I ended up realizing that, while I couldn't give it up completely, if I were judicious with my courses and book marketing, then I could make almost as much money just as a writer since I wouldn't need the revenue to keep those other businesses going.

I stopped my podcast. I stopped driving traffic to coaching and courses. I stopped doing editorial projects.

Whenever I see others suffering the same burnout I did, I think about what my friend and wife told me.

What if you just did the one thing you love instead of the hundred other things you think you need to do to keep the thing you love going?

What if you pared down to the essentials?

Would it allow you to put out more products and possibly, just maybe, cover the revenue from the things you're giving up?

If you can't cut completely, what if you cut out the low-margin activities in favor of a couple of high-margin ones?

What if instead of doing something else and funneling that money into your passion, you just did your passion?

Now, I was lucky that I could make that choice, and even then, I still maintain courses and do book marketing, but now I do them on my terms.

They now work for me instead of me working for them, and they are always in service to one goal: giving me more time to write.

It's been quite liberating, and I can focus almost all my energy on writing, allowing me to write more and do more of the thing I was put on this Earth to do.

Since I made that decision, I have written 11 books in the past 12 months.

I also spend a lot of time marketing myself, but as a writer, not as a guru or whatever else I was doing. Focusing on writing does not mean ONLY writing. To me, it means targeting activities that move my writing career forward, which includes marketing and sales.

This might not work for you, but I know almost everybody is dealing with some form of this, one way or another, so hopefully, it resonates.

We are taught that more is better, but that's not true. Growth for the sake of growth, without intentionality, is not better. Growth into something you don't want to be is not better. Busy for the sake of busyness isn't better.

SELF-PUBLISH WELL

A few weeks ago, I was on *The Dan Wickline Show,* and he asked me the very broad question of how to self-publish well and sell a lot of books. I thought I would give you my answer, fleshed out in a little more detail, because I quite liked it.

It really comes down to a couple of things.

1. MAKE SOMETHING GOOD

Your book HAS to be as good as anything the big publishers put out.

Somebody has to look at your book and not tell the difference between it and what Random House, Dark Horse, etc., put out. It needs to have YOUR flair, but it cannot be lacking in art, cover, story, or anything else.

You can sell books with subpar art/story, but if you want to sell A LOT of books, like make-a-career-out-of-it-level-of-books, your books HAVE to be of exceptional quality.

That means editorial, cover design, book design, story, blurb, everything needs to meet and, usually, beat the industrial average.

2. GET COMFORTABLE WITH REJECTION

Once you are an exceptional maker of things, you need to realize that for every 100 people you talk to, 99 will NOT be your ideal reader, so you need to get REALLY COMFORTABLE with rejection because you'll need to talk to literally hundreds of thousands of people to find an audience to jam with you. The more niche your work, the more people you need to speak with to find one who is into your work.

Just because somebody says NO doesn't mean your work is bad. It just means they aren't grokking what you put down.

This is why it's so important that your work be OBJECTIVELY GOOD, even if it is subjectively not somebody's jam.

3. NURTURE YOUR AUDIENCE

Once you have an audience, even a little one, you must fan those flames by making things FOR THEM. Yes, it's really fun to make other types of books and write whatever you want, but every time you write in a new genre, or format, you have to basically build that audience from scratch again. Since almost nobody will be a massive, runaway bestseller, even me, by the way, it behooves you to make things for the fans you have.

That doesn't mean writing in one series, but it does mean that when somebody buys something from you, they are very likely to buy something else you write if that book is part of the same taste profile.

That allows you to maximize the dollar of every fan, making your back catalog more valuable. If you are constantly writing in different genres, your fans will be less likely to consume your back catalog. The more congruent your work is, the more likely the majority of your fans will go back and consume that older stuff.

I didn't do this at the beginning of my career to my detriment. I was still making a living, but when I started doing this was when everything exploded.

4. CREATE A SIGNATURE SERIES

To make finding fans (which is expensive) cost-effective, you need a signature series, with A LOT of books in it that gives you an excellent ROI when you run ads or do marketing for it.

Ichabod, for instance, has three and will soon have four volumes. The Godsverse Chronicles has two graphic novels and seven books, which will expand to three graphic novels and eleven books by January 2022.

This means when somebody digs into that series, they can return A LOT of money, which also means I can spend a considerable amount of money and effort to find readers for that series.

On top of that, every time I launch one of those books, it's another opportunity to build buzz around the series, find new readers, and get existing fans excited, infusing new life into back catalog books with each new installment, and giving myself additional opportunities for readers to find my work.

Conversely, with a standalone, you only have that one book launch to get the book selling, and then it fizzles out unless the book happens to take off quickly. Most books do not take off the first time out of the gate, so having multiple chances to get a book selling increases your odds of success.

This is another reason standalone books are hard until you are established, at least because you do not make a lot of money from a reader if they only buy one book from you. People are unlikely to read through the rest of your catalog when you write single, unconnected books compared to when you have a series.

Almost all successful authors have a series that keeps finding readers over time, allowing their publisher to spend money because the readthrough is high.

A good guideline is to make your signature series at least a million words for books and a minimum of 10-12 issues for comics.

I started making good money before having a signature series, but once you have one, marketing and advertising become far more cost-effective, and it just compounds with every subsequent book.

Once you have a signature series working for you, you can write standalones, or try to funnel people to your other works, but having one is so vital that it's almost impossible to exist without one.

It also helps readers with word of mouth, as they can talk up your series and refer people to it. I have learned how important it is to make it easy for your readers to talk you up over time. Referrals are a huge part of a successful author career.

And there you go.

Make something great that is of equal quality to the big publishing houses. Become comfortable with rejection. Keep your books in a consistent genre/tone to increase the value of your backlist. Design a signature series (a million words or so) that you can market perpetually and keep finding new readers.

One final note. Even if you do everything right, you will have books that fail to live up to expectations and others that outperform expectations. That is just a part of doing this work.

MY BET

My bet as a creative has always been pretty simple:

I am not lucky enough to make one thing and make it blow up and become massively successful. I am good enough, though, to make many different things and have a few of them make a splash based on the sheer volume of my material alone.

I know other creatives who have doubled down on one single project, or universe, and ridden it until the project paid off. In some cases, it has, but in many more cases, well, they end up working for years on a project that didn't move their career forward.

My bet is the opposite of theirs. I believe that with enough projects out in the public zeitgeist, some are bound to catch fire. Even if I don't know which ones will ignite, I know the odds are on my side if I keep making new things. Additionally, I am smart enough to figure out how to bring people to my work and determined enough to keep at it even when everybody else gives up.

My job, then, has always been to make the most high-quality things possible in as short an amount of time as I could reasonably do so to see which ones resonate while not spending too much time or resources on any one project, knowing that it will likely not catch fire. By assuming nothing will catch fire, I try to spend the least amount of time and resources on anything, making it easier to break even if something fizzles.

This does not mean I cheap out on projects. It means that I focus on creating the best product possible on a fixed budget. This might be writing a 30,000-word novel instead of a 90,000-word one because it can be written in a third of the time and cost significantly less to edit, or it might mean building a website on the back of another site until it shows revenue. The goal is always, "how do I create a great product with limited time and resources?"

When a project becomes a success, I focus more attention and resources on it moving forward. Otherwise, my job has always been to put as many projects into the world as possible without risking too much on any one bet until they start paying off. Where I end up spending money is on improving the overall chances of all my projects instead of any single one in particular.

It's not sexy or glamorous. However, a career full of projects that break even, punctuated once in a while with hits, isn't a bad way to build a career, it turns out. In the end, if nothing else, I have a career full of projects to look back on with pride.

RIVALS

I went to college at the University of Maryland. We HATED Duke.

A HATRED so deep you couldn't see the bottom. Our school motto was SCREW DUKE.

It was insane and irrational, but so was most of college.

One day I was having dinner with my cousin who went to Duke, whom I hadn't seen since she started.

So I was ready to needle her about it.

"So what's it like now that we're rivals?" I asked.

"We're not rivals," she replied.

"What are you talking about? We hate Duke. They are definitely our rivals."

"Maybe we are your rivals, but you aren't ours."

That has stuck with me for years as a reminder that the person taking up your brain space probably isn't thinking about you at all...ever.

DOING EVERYTHING

I speak at a lot of conferences. I added it to my arsenal this year, and it's going well.

I also have a weekly blog, a twice-weekly podcast, a strong social media presence, exhibit at dozens of cons a year around the country, and run a publishing company. Even with that, I'm still able to attend to clients and get projects finished.

If I looked at myself from five years ago, I would hyperventilate. I never thought that was possible—like ever. I was struggling even to get a few hundred words a day written.

Yet, now I do it without a second thought. That's because I've had time to figure it all out. Everybody you respect has spent years building a following, learning how business works, figuring out how to add revenue channels, and making it all seem effortless. You need to quit comparing yourself to them. You'll get there if you work at it.

I see people just starting out worried because they can't do as much as me. They ask me for my secret, and it's very simple.

I didn't do it all at once.

What you see is a decades-long culmination of me becoming great at one thing, then systematizing it so I can do it with the least time commitment possible, then adding something else, and becoming great at that. Meanwhile, I'm cutting out stuff that doesn't work. So just like the robots in the *Matrix* when they destroy Zion for the fifth time, I am getting exceedingly good at doing what works for me.

When I started, though, I didn't know what worked. I tried everything. I was doing things that wasted my time with no gain. I was spinning my wheels more than I was being productive. I was like a duck, kicking furiously to stay afloat.

But that's what you do as a young creator. Like a child, you don't know the stove is hot, and the dog is friendly. So you touch everything until you figure it out. Parents, like coaches, can and should guide you, but you have to be the one learning what works for you.

And, like a child, you grow over time. You learn what works and what doesn't. You discover who likes your work and who doesn't. You understand your strengths and weaknesses. Then you can double down on those and cut out the ones that don't work for you.

And that's where I see a lot of young creators going wrong. They think they can get the following with mediocre content if they have several dozen social media profiles. They want quantity over quality.

However, it can't happen overnight. First-time authors do become best sellers, but that's a fluke. You can't base your career on a fluke any more than you can base your life on winning the lottery.

So I recommend focusing on creating great content first. Write or draw or bake or whatever it is you do. Get great at that one thing first.

Of course, you will have a blog or a podcast, and social media is key, but while you are sucky at a thing or mediocre at a thing, don't worry about not having a big audience. Don't worry that you aren't David Baldacci. Worry about being great at being a content creator.

Before you can start supercharging your audience, you MUST be able to give them great content they want to see.

Before people ask you to speak at their shows you need to have a track record of success they can Google. Before success, you need the work.

There is a process of growth that comes over time. You get better at stuff you work hard at improving. You can't help but get better.

Whenever I teach people how to make money on their work, my first statement is always, "This is all assuming you have great content. If you don't have great content already, then you are in the wrong place."

Because great content is the barometer. Everybody has great content. Everybody from Tim Ferris down to Stephen King and me and so on are going after audience eyeballs. We already create great content.

But if you have great content, it's about doing it better and quicker so you can start building your audience.

GOOD GUY

A tip for you today. While watching TV or a movie, write down the hero's journey of the villain. What would their movie look like? How could they be the hero? How could the hero be the villain?

This is a trick you can and should bring to your own stories. If you can find a way to make the villain the hero of their story, it will be easier to make them compelling and interesting.

You don't have to agree with their arc, but you should be able to understand it in detail. The best antagonist and villain characters are built to be the hero of their own story.

You can even gamify this with friends and try to develop the most compelling story among you for a character.

Extra credit: take minor characters and write about their journey. How is the baker that only appears in one scene the hero of their journey?

Rich worlds are full of characters who are the heroes of their own stories.

MY DOGS

I have two dogs. I love them both to death. There is an adorable, regal, aloof one named Nala and a small, yappy attention-seeker named Cheyenne.

Here's the thing. They both want my attention. They want it more than anything…except my wife's attention. They really love my wife's attention.

But Nala doesn't ask for it. She'll sometimes look doe-eyed and wonder why I'm not giving her attention. She'll curl up and look wounded that I'm not paying attention to her, but she will never come up and ask for it.

My small dog, on the other hand…there's nothing she won't do for attention. She will barrel into people. She will jump on your lap even if you're not sitting down. She will jump on the back of your foot, causing you to trip and fall. She'll lick your face while you're doing yoga.

There is nothing she won't do to get cuddly. She is aggressively cuddly, which is the only appropriate term for her. She is relentless with her snuggles.

I don't think she likes cuddling more than Nala. I think she is just vehement that she's going to get hers. She doesn't care if Nala gets pets too, but she's gonna get hers.

What it tells me about business is that to get what you want, you need to announce yourself! You have to tell people you want their business and get in front of them. You have to be relentless about it, otherwise, somebody else will be.

While both my dogs love us equally, and while we love both our dogs equally, one sleeps next to my wife and naps with me while the other one lies twenty feet away, pining for our attention.

And all because Nala doesn't ask and Cheyenne does. So if you want something in business, you have to ask for it. You have to be aggressively cuddly about it.

STAYING POSITIVE

The world is tough for everybody. Nobody has an easy go of it.

But we, as writers, are one of few that chose to take our lot in life and make it exponentially more miserable due to the constant worry, rejection, and disappointment that comes with being an entrepreneur.

Here are a couple of strategies I use to stay positive.

It's not easy for me. I'm not a positive person. Perhaps I should rename this, how to keep going, instead of how to stay positive.

1. **Savor the little victories.** Whether it's a good review from a friend, a positive note from a possible agent, selling a book at a con, or breaking even for the first time after a decade of writing, there are little victories. All of those little victories will add up over time.
2. **Don't forget how far you've come.** Whenever I'm with my friends, and we start complaining, I always say, "Yeah, but if we told us two years ago this would be where we'd be now, we would flip out". You are probably doing better than you think and certainly better than you were two years ago.
3. **Understand you are never where you want to be.** No matter where you climb, you will want the next rung.

It's just who we are. First, we want to finish a book. Then we want an agent. Then we want a publisher. Then we want a release. Then we want a best seller. Then we want a book deal for the next one. Then we want to make enough to quit our job. Then we want speaking engagements. It never ends.

4. **Get out of the house.** Look, who doesn't love their home? Nothing is better than walking around in underoos and not needing to impress anybody. But connections are important. And being outside is important. Taking a break from worrying is important. Breaking up the routine is important.

5. **Never stick with something that makes you miserable.** I know not everybody is in the position to quit a bad job, move to a new town, or leave their crappy relationship, but if you even plan to do so, it will help. Life is short, and we only have one go around, so being miserable is even worse. It took almost a decade of building and struggling to form Wannabe Press, but there was always a plan. And even the plan made it all bearable.

NOT EVERYONE

Not everyone will love your writing, even if it is absolutely off-the-charts amazing.

Moreover, it is selfish to believe everyone SHOULD like your stuff, especially because YOU don't like everything you see.

This whole game, the whole of it, is making something amazing that you believe in with your whole heart and suffering through a million people saying no so that you can find a few people who say yes.

That's it.

The quicker and more efficiently you do that, the more successful you will be, but even the most successful person in the world has more people who have said no to them than have said yes.

If you want proof of this, read any Goodreads review, or browse through Metacritic, Rotten Tomatoes, or any other site that aggregates reviews of anything.

There is no consensus on what is good or bad, and in this world of fractured attention, you don't have to get most people to like it.

All you need is a fraction of a fraction of a fraction of them.

HOW TO DESIGN A SIGNATURE SERIES

Somebody asked me about planning a series the other day, so I thought I would give you my thoughts, having written three major ones in my career (The Godsverse Chronicles, *Ichabod Jones: Monster Hunter*, and The Obsidian Spindle Saga).

Before I get started, I will tell you these are my opinions. You might hate them all, but I don't care. You can plan a series any way you like, but this is how I do it and what works for me.

I will also specifically be talking about a signature series, which is one that has a million+ words in it and spans across several books. For comics, this is at least a maxi-series with 12+ issues.

First and foremost, there are many reasons to write a book, but writing a signature series is to make money and define your career. There are plenty of smaller series and standalone books which you can write for fun, but a series is about pulling in the type of money that allows you to do this full-time.

It's an absolute mind-numbing amount of work and stress. There is no other reason to do a signature series than to define your career and create something with long-term sales potential.

Here are the main questions you should ask before starting a signature series.

1. WHAT GENRE DO I WANT TO BE KNOWN FOR?

A good signature series might span many subgenres, but it needs to clearly be defined by a single main genre. Readers are looking for a specific genre when they search for a book, at least the first book in a series, and the more tightly you can define that genre, the better your sales will be, and since signature series are mainly about both short and long term sales, defining your series well is critical for success.

There are five main genres that indies can hope to succeed in, which are ranked in order of probability of success, as defined by the popularity of the genre in the self-published space.

1. **Romance** - the most popular genre by far, and it accounts for more book sales than all other genres combined.
2. **Thriller/Mystery/Crime** - easily the second most popular genre, far ahead of all the others, save romance.
3. **Science Fiction** - the surge of sales from military sci-fi has vaulted sci-fi past fantasy in total sales.
4. **Fantasy** - close behind science fiction.
5. **Horror** - far behind all other categories listed.

Now, there are many subgenres and categories underneath each of them. You can have epic fantasy or urban fantasy, military sci-fi or alien invasion, contemporary romance or historical romance, but you need to define your main genre, the one that readers will place you for the rest of your career.

If you write in another genre, find a way to make it feel like one of these genres because those are the ones that sell.

Remember, though, that this is the series you will be known for and what you expect new readers to pick up first when they hear about you, so don't choose a genre unless you intend to write in it for a long time and are comfortable with the majority of readers knowing you are that kind of writer.

It is very hard to change a career trajectory once you have a signature series, so only go into one once you know for sure the type of thing you want to be known for by the majority of people who find your work.

That might take 5-10+ books before you figure that out, or maybe you already know it, but this is a big commitment. Don't go into it lightly.

2. WHAT SUBGENRE/TROPES WILL DEFINE THIS SERIES?

Every genre has some enduring tropes and subgenres that are timeless, and you will want to choose a timeless trope for your series as you want them to be bought for the rest of your life and beyond.

For instance, paranormal romance shifters or vampires will probably endure for at least the next decade.

The same thing with fantasy and fairy tales or dragon riders.

Military sci-fi and space opera also dominate the sci-fi charts, so sometimes a small niche subgenre is responsible for an oversized part of a genre's success, and writing in any other subgenre would be folly.

Once you have your genre, it's essential to pick a subgenre that is robust and enduring as you want to make sales on this series for years into the future. Even if the sales are middling at the beginning, a signature series gains value over time, as every reader who sticks with it buys more books the longer the series goes on.

3. WHAT KIND OF SERIES IS THIS GOING TO BE?

There are a few types of series that endure.

1. **Serialized series** - This is something like Mistborn or Game of Thrones. The books end on cliffhangers and need to be read in the correct order to make sense. The Obsidian Spindle Saga is a serialized series.
2. **Episodic series** - Mark Dawson and most thriller/crime books are episodic and star the same set of characters, but with different crimes to solve every book.
3. **Anthology series** - Christopher Moore makes anthology series, as do most romance writers. An anthology series follows different characters in every book, but in the same world, often with ancillary characters becoming lead characters and people showing up in multiple books. The Godsverse Chronicles is an anthology series.

Each of these has its positives and negatives. Serialized stories are great because they have an immediate hook to read the next book, but people sometimes get pissed about cliffhangers.

Episodic stories are standalone, which people like, but because of that finality, people are less likely to continue to the next book, so you need to give them a reason to keep moving from book to book with an underlying story that bubbles under the surface for several books, or at least an epilogue that teases something to come in the next book.

Anthology series are great because each book has new characters,.But because of that, people are even less likely to finish than in other types of series as every book has new characters they have to fall in love with. However, there are many more chances for people to fall in love, too, and get hooked on a series.

4. WHAT IS THE POV OF THE MAIN CHARACTER(S)?

For me, questions 3 and 4 often go in tandem because I often need the character's voice before I figure out the series.

1. **Third person omniscient** - This is a wide view of the world, where the narrator can see everything and knows everything about the world. The narrator talks in the third person about the characters they are watching.
2. **Third person limited** - Like omniscient, this is about talking about the characters the narrator is watching, but they don't know everything or anything aside from what they are viewing at this moment.
3. **First person** - We are inside the character's head, talking in the first person.
4. **Second person** - I haven't seen this much, but N.K. Jemison did it so beautifully that I have to add it. The narrator is talking about a character using YOU. I don't recommend this type of series unless you are really

confident in your writing and already have an audience.

5. HOW MANY MAIN CHARACTERS WILL THERE BE?

I'm tipping my hat here, but I have a REALLY hard time writing a series from a single character's point of view. It's a LOT of words to stick with one character, so my books either have multiple POVs between the chapters (4-5 with The Obsidian Spindle) or are anthology series, where each book follows a different character.

Even with *Ichabod Jones: Monster Hunter,* which was a single-person POV, it was hard not to cut away to different characters all the time.

Even if you are doing an anthology series, you need to get some sense of the scope of the book series and who will be interacting with who over the course of it.

With romance, the king of anthology series, you will often follow each member of a family, or a workplace, or a dorm, or something, so you have to design each of those characters from the beginning, as they will keep appearing in multiple books.

6. WHAT IS THE HOOK INTO YOUR SERIES?

The most important single element of the writing process is the hook into your series. How will they be introduced to your signature series? It needs to be in such a way that slowly brings them up to speed and parcels out the important elements over time. Remember, this is a million-word series in a sprawling world. The instinct is to use a firehose to tell people about your world, but you need to dole the information out over time.

For The Obsidian Spindle Saga, I chose to use Rose as the character who would introduce the audience to the world. When she falls into a diabetic coma, she wakes up in the Dream Realm, and we use her eyes to see everything that happens and then fill in the world with the perspectives of Chelle, Red, and the Wicked Witch, Nimue.

Sometimes you will get it wrong, too. With The Godsverse Chronicles, the first book has always been And Death Followed Behind Her. However, it's an awkward first book, starting in an Apocalypse and then cutting 10,000 years into the future.

I chose to write a new introduction book to the series, and that one introduction became four books that eased readers into the series before it got all nutso on them. Those books will be released in January 2020, and I think they are a better way to ease people into the series and make them understand the world.

It's not wrong to go big, crazy, and wild with your series, but give people time to understand it and parcel the big changes out over time. The audience will follow you as long as you give them a reason and the time to get acquainted with your world.

I recommend only introducing one new setting/world per book. My rule has been to spend a book understanding a single setting/conflict, introducing new settings/conflict at the beginning of the next book, and ratcheting the conflict up more and more with each passing book in the series.

The problem with *And Death Followed Behind Her* wasn't the writing. It was in introducing too much too fast before the reader could understand and appreciate the series. The longer your series goes, the more latitude a reader will give you.

7. WHAT IS YOUR UNIQUE SELLING PROPOSITION?

Okay, so we've talked about falling into the tropes of a genre already, but a signature series also has to have something unique about it that will carry people and interest through for the long haul.

How do you take certain tropes and turn them on their head? How do you take everything that we know about a genre and turn it on its head?

8. WHERE WILL I BE PRIMARILY SELLING THIS SERIES?

A book that will sell on Amazon will be designed much differently than one which you plan on selling on Kickstarter and conventions.

That is because Amazon is based around the mass market, and the taste of the mass market is way different than people who come to conventions.

Everything from the blurb to the cover to the tropes you use will change based on whether you are hand-selling your book or running ads for it as well.

From here, designing a series is a lot like designing any single book, but you have to make sure your world and characters are robust enough to support several books in the same series, so it takes longer.

Usually, it takes me 1-2 years to design a new series because I need to find all sorts of new and interesting pieces for the universe that the series will revolve around and conflict interesting enough to bubble over for several books.

Remember, this is your SIGNATURE series and the thing you want to be known for the long haul. It's the thing fans will tell their friends about to get them into your work and what you will be running ads around for the next several years, at least, if not the next several decades.

One last thing I want to talk about is how series build on each other. Even though this is a signature series, you will likely have a few in your career, and each one will build on the next.

For me, I took a lot of the elements of The Godsverse Chronicles and smoothed them out in The Obsidian Spindle Saga while giving my own spin on new things.

The goal, for me, is to expand my audience with every series so that more and more people find me over time, pulling them into a deeper and deeper relationship with me.

PRODUCTIVITY

The biggest "secret" I've learned to be productive is this:

You have to be okay with the fact that you will sometimes be at your worst.

Not only will that chapter not be good enough, it will be awful, but you have to keep going anyway.

You have to get comfortable with the idea that some projects will not be your best work or even good work by your standards.

Some days it will suck.

However, with that secret comes another one.

By doing the work every day for years, your worst will still be better than 99.9% of people.

Your mediocre will be breathtaking.

Your best will be mind-blowing.

By doing the work every day, you train yourself to do the work, and by doing the work, you get better at doing the work. Your eye gets better, your brain gets better, and you get better.

But you have to be okay with the fact that some days will be your worst because if some days are your best, then you have to have your worst days too.

Those terrible days can be smoothed over in editing or, in a pinch, by your editor. Sometimes you might have to do extra edits to get it to the point where you feel it's good enough.

Maybe it won't be good enough, ever, and you shelve it. Luckily, that doesn't happen to me very much anymore, but it used to happen a lot.

But that's because by doing the work, I got better at doing the work and knowing what kinds of things light me up.

I got very good at knowing what a "Russell Nohelty" project is and what will give me a full-body yes.

Everything else is a no.

By doing the work for so long, I learned how to know when the work is good enough.

But some days, I'm still at my worst.

That is part of it.

TWISTED

People get it twisted.

I didn't choose to be indie. I'm not Scott Snyder. I'm not Brandon Sanderson.

They chose to go indie.

The choice existed because mainstream publishers wanted their work. They paid big money for their work. They would shovel work their way forever, and those authors chose to put out books independently in the face of big contracts anyway.

That is a choice.

My choice was either to publish independently or not publish at all.

This is the choice most writers will face.

The discussion is always about whether an author will choose to publish with a company or self-publish, but that is a false choice. For most of us, the choice is whether we will self-publish or not publish at all.

Framing the choice that way makes the decision quite clear. I chose to publish. The only option presented to me was to publish myself and take my career into my own hands.

I take that decision seriously. I formed a company. I hire artists, editors, and designers.

But I didn't "decide" to be indie.

I decided to publish.

And indie was my only choice to get my work out there. Even now, mainstream publishers do not want my work, so I put it out myself to this day. I still don't have a choice, even after all the success that I've had, at least not in the way most people talk about it.

In the same way, writers often fall out with publishers or "go cold", and the contracts stop coming.

In that scenario, there is also no choice between publishing with a company or self-publishing.

The choice is "wait and hope somebody takes a chance on me" or self-publish.

That is not to say people don't get good publishing contracts and don't go on to have amazing careers, but there are mercilessly few of them.

Yes, it happens.

You could be the next Veronica Roth or Malcolm Gladwell. You absolutely could set the world on fire with your book.

And then you will have a choice.

But for most writers, there is no choice, and I wish people would stop framing it that way

IT MATTERS

I had a hard time for a long time when the pandemic began trying to write anything.

In fact, I wrote a book in January and another in February of 2020, but then I didn't get another book done until the end of May, which means I took two whole months to do nothing because I simply couldn't process how writing could be important when the world was falling apart.

Then a funny thing happened.

I realized that the worse I felt, the more I disappeared into movies, TV, books, games, and other things.

Those things became my salvation, and I realized then that while my writing might not fix the world, it could give some solace to people dealing with it.

It's not much, maybe, but for people suffering through the world, it might be the only thing they have to hang on to, these silly things we make.

That realization led to one of the most productive times in my life, where I have written 16 books in 15 months, and easily the most words I have ever written in one stretch in my whole life, with 1.1 million words written in that time compared to 800k when I wrote my first massive 20-month book marathon from June 2017-February 2019.

It matters because it matters to someone.

WHY SHOULD PEOPLE CARE?

WSPC.

Why should people care?

It's not just because you made something. For a very small group of people, it is, but not most people. Not enough people to make a career.

It's because of how it makes them feel and being able to link a positive emotional reaction to your project.

It has to be personal to you because it has to be personal to them, or no one will care.

I see it over and over again.

It is absolutely enough that you made a thing. That's stellar. Honest and truly, you could stop there, and I would think you were incredible. Do you know how hard it is to make something from nothing?

So hard.

However, if you want other people to buy that thing, you must link your work to an emotional reaction. It has to make them feel a way, deep down.

You must dig deep and make them feel it, often multiple times in multiple ways.

There are many ways to get that response, but you have to elicit it, or you are dead in the water.

Otherwise, you will keep launching to crickets.

It's probably not your work that is the problem. It's almost always the way you talk about it, how often you talk about it, who you talk about it to, and/or how many people you talk about it to.

Solve those four problems, and you solve the whole game.

ESCAPE VELOCITY

People, especially at the beginning of their careers, talk about how they haven't accomplished anything, and they feel they never will.

What they don't understand is that a career gathers velocity over time. If you keep at it, eventually, you will break through and start being very, very productive, partially because you figure out how to write in your style (which is the hardest part of the writing journey) and partly because people trust you with more and more things over time.

For instance, I have been at this writing game for a long time, since 2006, and yet, I had the most productive time of my career in the last two years, over 14 years after I started writing.

How productive?

Nearly HALF of my entire writing output for my life has happened in the past two years (52/109 total projects)

Yes, I wrote a ton in the past few years, but it was in the 14th and 15th years of my writing career.

So, if you aren't there yet, that's okay. It takes a long time to get to that point. I know it did for me. In fact, it's so much work that it will take two more years for it all to come out.

Yes, I could sit on my hands for two years producing nothing, and I would still be launching more than ten books a year through 2024.

Maybe you'll get there fast, but maybe it will take you over a decade, but if you keep going, you will get there.

UNIVERSAL FANTASY

A good first step in understanding WSPC (Why Should People Care) is to define the universal fantasy people get from your work.

Oh, you don't know about universal fantasies? Read *Seven Figure Fiction* right now.

No, this isn't just for fantasy authors. It's for EVERY author, no matter what you write (even if you write non-fiction).

Do not write another book without absorbing it into your bones.

It's probably the most crucial piece of book marketing in the last year, aside from my books with Monica Leonelle and our solo books, of course.

But honestly, it might be more important because our books discuss how you can make sales and the levers you can pull, but that book gets to the core of why good book marketing works.

It basically boils down to this: What escapist fantasy are readers getting from your work? What singular need in the reader's psyche are you fulfilling with your fiction?

Mine is easy. It's empowerment.

People for years have told me they love my work because the characters have agency in a cruel world, and they use that agency to affect change.

It might seem obvious to me now, but it wasn't until I read that book; it all clicked, and I turned my marketing toward that aim: finding people who wanted fantasy that empowers them.

Not only that, but it is a guide for every book I write. Does it deliver on that Universal Fantasy or not?

Using that one word, I can very easily tailor ALL my messaging to that end and drill down on the fact that the thing you will get out of my work is a feeling of agency in a chaotic world.

Bad guys are beaten. Good guys win. The cruel world is bent to the will of justice. It's noblebright fantasy; I just didn't know it then.

There are all sorts of universal fantasies out there (which is why you should read the book), but you need to figure out YOURS.

I have for years told people all sorts of things to get started, but now I tell authors one thing when it comes to marketing.

WHAT IS THE UNIVERSAL FANTASY YOUR WORK FULFILLS?

This can be different per series, but generally, once you have a couple of series, you will find that the UF of your series is pretty consistent because it's at the core of all your work.

If a long time fan doesn't like one of your books, especially if you have a wide catalog, it's probably because you didn't deliver the universal fantasy you are known for as an author.

Once you have that piece and figure out what people will GAIN from reading your work, you are on the path to showing them why they should care about your work because you are finally answering the most important question in marketing.

What's in it for ***THEM?***

PIVOT

People often tell me that I pivot to new lines of business very well and ask me how I do it.

I figured I would write down what I've learned about pivoting over the years. I think it comes down to a few factors.

1. GETTING PUNCHED

There is no substitute for experience. If you don't want to get punched in the mouth yourself, then at least hire a coach who can see all the red flags coming and steer you away from them.

I can't tell you how many months of my life would have been saved by having somebody who had already been there to tell me something was a bad idea.

Of course, I'm stubborn, so I don't know if I would have listened, but I regret not having that when I was younger. I did have a good group of friends who were on the same journey as me to bounce ideas off of, though, which was helpful.

It used to take me a lot longer to pivot, though, because I didn't have the experience to see what was coming.

2. PLAN

Two examples here. With Wannabe Press, we were planning to be more reliant on online sales in 2017, but that plan took three years to implement. It took hundreds, maybe thousands of hours of planning to position ourselves to make that happen.

We began implementing our plan in 2020, a couple of months before the pandemic, we were prepared to weather it when it came. Even then, it nearly tore us apart, but we were more ready than almost anyone around us.

Second, Monica and I had already run a campaign for our Kickstarter book and had a beta cohort of our Accelerator that allowed us to test all our theories before launching our program. There was some success, and we were ready to move forward eventually, so when we saw the Brandon Sanderson campaign, it allowed us to leap on it.

From there, we've spent the last couple of months building the infrastructure around it. Now, we're working on cornering the market, but it would never have happened if we hadn't prepared long in advance to make that pivot when the opportunity presented itself.

In both cases, we had a long-term plan that could be shortened or lengthened depending on a host of factors. Planning 2-5 steps ahead and having contingency plans in case things went wrong or right was essential for our pivot.

3. DEVELOP SKILLS

I've been a one-man show for most of my adult life, and because of that, I've learned a lot about how to run a business. I'm an expert at book publishing and Kickstarter, but I also have a degree in journalism, which allowed me to master virtual conferences, podcasts, and about a hundred other things, from accounting to contract negotiation.

All of that allowed me to pivot all over the place because I dug deep into every aspect of business and learned how it worked to build a solid foundation under myself.

I sold courses for years before the Accelerator blew up, appeared at hundreds of conventions, and both guested on and hosted tons of podcasts before partnering with Monica.

There is a curiosity needed to pivot well and specifically for exploring things that might be helpful in the future, even if it's not helpful now.

The main reason I can pivot well is that I explored every avenue, and even though I abandoned most of them, when it became relevant again, I brushed off those skills and could move on them almost immediately.

4. TRUST

Even though I know a lot about a lot of things, the thing I know most is what needs to be offloaded so I can focus on my own zone of genius.

I do not do my own taxes, edit my own books, do my own covers, proofread my own stuff, edit my own podcast, or...well, you get the point. Monica is even better at this than I am, and she's taught me a lot about offloading things to other people.

While I know how to do those things, I know what I don't want to do and what I don't do well enough to matter.

Knowing the landscape allows me to speak intelligently about many subjects and then offload the work to contractors, giving them a good sense of what needs to get done, so it gets done right the first time.

5. DON'T BE PRECIOUS

Most things service you until they don't, and when they stop servicing me, I jettison them quickly.

Moreso, I notice when things are not servicing me well in advance and that allows me to abandon them before they crash-land at my feet.

Whether it was my Complete Creative podcast, running author marketing for clients, or ending series before the bottom dropped out, I have always been able to tell the warning signs (making less money/having few listens with each installment, fewer social media engagements, etc.), and pivot away from them.

I've also been able to integrate new things that serviced me into my arsenal seamlessly because I planned for a long time before I pulled the trigger on anything, making sure it fit with my audience.

I'm usually a year, or so ahead of my slate, so I can move my marketing in whatever way I need to make things seem natural.

Most people are weighed down, especially after years of doing this work, with the past, especially things that don't work or barely break even. They keep writing that series that barely breaks even or keep servicing that client who is more trouble than they are worth.

I have found that being able to disassociate the work from the marketing has helped me incredibly in being able to pivot to new things.

This also means that you should liberally cut things you are developing which don't work for you. At the beginning of the pandemic, I was developing a membership called Happy Pivot about pivoting. After developing it for months, I realized it was too far out of my lane and abandoned it.

I spent a lot of time on it, and most people would probably have kept going, but I do not believe in the sunk cost fallacy. If something won't serve me in the long term, then no matter when I figure that out, it needs to be cut and abandoned or integrated into something that will work in the long term.

Notice, though, long term doesn't mean forever. I hesitate even to say long term because something could service me for one launch, and if it scratches an itch in me, then it's worth doing, as long as I'm ready to cut ties with it shortly after and people who buy it have a good experience with the product. I have a whole suite of books and courses I only launched once that did just that, but they are not the kind of thing I build my business on or count on past that one singular launch.

6. PIVOT

Yes, some things need time to finish, like a long series, but that doesn't mean you can't be pivoting in other areas of your life/business.

You can keep one thing dragging along with one hand while pivoting with the other.

This year I'm spending my time mostly shuttering three series (Godsverse Chronicles, *Ichabod Jones: Monster Hunter,* and *Cthulhu is Hard to Spell*). However, at the same time, Monica and I spun up a whole new business, launched a podcast, and are in the middle of a second Kickstarter launch for our series.

This is mostly possible because those series were complete in 2021, so I could focus on launching them instead of writing them, but you don't have to pivot with your whole life. You can keep certain things going, spin down other things, and spin up still more, allowing you to keep pivoting.

Because that's the biggest thing I've learned--there is ALWAYS a pivot. The reason people aren't very good at it is that they are waiting for the one perfect pivot, but it's usually, almost always, a series of little pivots that slide in and out of your life.

The better you can get at constantly being in flux, the less anything can knock you down because you'll be ready to pivot and allow it to flow through you.

Finally, this life is long, and you can always learn how to pivot better, even if you're not great at it now.

ROCKSTAR

I have had a lot of conversations after revealing the depth of my chronic illnesses that have gone something like this:

- **Person:** Sucks your body is broken, dude. I'm just gonna go hard until I become a superstar, and then they'll do it for me . So, I won't have the same problem as you.
- **Me:** ...
- **Me:** ...
- **Me:** "I can't even tell you all the things wrong with that statement."

So, I figured I would clear this up once and for all with a harsh truth.

You will never be a superstar.

It won't happen.

There are maybe 1,000 rockstar creators like that in all of publishing, and I'm being exceedingly generous. The odds are so minuscule and statistically insignificant that it's not even worth examining.

I'm talking about people that draw a crowd wherever they go, who can greenlight any project, and who are known throughout the industry as the surefire bets. I'm talking about your Neil Gaimans, Ta-Nehisi Coateses, and Nora

Robertses. People who are so successful can write their own tickets and barely lift a finger to get a million sales from their name alone.

Most of those creators broke out years ago and are living off that fame still to this day. Fewer than a handful break through to that elite status in any given year.

Even if you happen to be a superstar for a year or two, it's harder to remain a superstar than to become one. Most stars burn bright and fade fast.

Could it happen?

Yes, theoretically, but in practice, it will never happen to anyone and is impossible to plan for, even if it did. There is so much luck involved that striving for it is a lesson in futility.

More importantly, the publishing industry sells the idea of becoming a superstar to sell all sorts of awful things while making creators feel bad about themselves when they do everything right and don't break like their idols.

Simply pursuing that as your goal is toxic to your mental and physical health.

Besides, even publishers don't know which authors will become superstars.

They are using a scattershot approach, launching a bunch of books and knowing one will rise above the rest, even if they can't predict which one will be a hit.

If they can't even predict which author will become a superstar, then what hope do you have of doing so? None.

That is not to say you can't be successful. You can be very successful in publishing without being a superstar. You can plan for success. You can't plan for superstardom because too much luck is involved in being plucked from obscurity and anointed as the golden child.

You can be very, very successful, though…

However, if you're just very successful, you'll be doing it all yourself. You'll be doing 99% of your marketing. You'll be lugging books to shows. You'll be booking your own flights...

...and people will tell you to suck it up and be grateful for the privilege of getting ignored by them because you are living the good life.

Now, here is a sober fact...

...nobody in publishing, save the very, very tippy top, lead the good life.

There is no money in publishing for almost anyone. I know people writing for Marvel who are on food stamps. The average salary for a published writer is less than $10,000.

Those not struggling are doing illustration commissions or have some other way to bring in money, like writing on tv shows, because working in publishing is no way to a thriving bank account.

That's not to say that there are not people in publishing with thriving bank accounts, just that they are the rare exception.

I do very well in publishing, and usually, it's just enough to rob Peter to pay Paul so I can get from one month to the next. Even if I have a good launch, it slowly whittles down over the next few months until I'm right back to where I started.

Publishing is a war of attrition. For most titles, you're trying to break even so you can live long enough to find a hit that can pay for the rest of your line.

That is not to say working in publishing is not a worthy goal, but if you are hoping to be magically plucked from the masses and given the diamond key to the golden palace, then you should know...

...the diamond is really cubic zirconia, and that castle is only plated in gold which flakes off at the slightest touch. It's still a castle, which is cool, but underneath that beautiful veneer is a lot of rotten wood and cracked stone.

For most creators, it will be a full-time job to keep it from crumbling. It might not be worth killing yourself to inherit such a castle.

After all, your health is all you have. You're trapped in this singular body, and when it fails, that's all you get.

I'm not saying, don't go hard if this is your passion. I think running hard until you find success is extremely helpful in the beginning, but that effort will bring in lesser returns with every passing year.

You have to change your approach all the time, which is one thing that is utterly exhausting about doing this work.

If you want to barrel through until you are a superstar, you will be barreling through forever, and your body can't handle that.

Not to mention, your mental health will suffer irreparably if you don't get there, which you won't.

It's much better to say, "I'm going hard for x time", or "I'm going hard until I have this much work done", or "let's test this and see if it works, and then redirect if not".

If you have hypotheses to test and markers to hit along the way to prove your concepts, then it's easier to shift your plans as new information becomes available.

My deadline was five years of backbreaking days and nights away from my wife before I couldn't do it anymore.

I had that deadline in my head from the start of my journey, and I discussed it with my wife constantly.

It was never about running forever. It was always until "X point and/or Y conditions" were met. When those conditions were met, I assessed the effectiveness of my assumptions and made new ones based on what I learned.

I presented the plan to my wife at regular intervals for her comments, too. I had to defend my plans like people defend their dissertations, and we had to agree on the next steps together.

During those years, I wanted to finish a body of work large enough that I would never have to run hard again. I now have a bookshelf full of my work, with more on the way. It took over a decade, but I got there.

Still, I'm not sure even that will bring long-term success beyond what I have already achieved. I constantly worry it will all go away with the snap of a finger.

But I have no choice but to pivot because I mentally can't do a book a month anymore, and I physically can't do shows anymore, putting me at an impasse.

I'm on sabbatical right now because the thought of writing ever again fills me with so much dread I have panic attacks when I open a new word document. I need time off because I did so much damage to myself over the past several years.

Some people have better stamina than me and still run the circuit after 20 years. Some artists, especially those who don't have books to lug around the world, can do it more easily than I can, but for me, it was those years and that goal of amassing a body of work.

But for all that, I am paying the price for those years on the grind now.

You can't guess how your body will handle the stress.

I didn't know I would have overlapping chronic conditions that would zap my strength. I also don't know how many of them presented because of how I worked myself in the past.

I wish you nothing but the best of health, but for your mental sanity, do not risk it all trying to become a superstar...

...and don't agree to run hard forever.

I know the dream seems worth it, and it is a very worthy goal to be the best in your field, but it's just a job at the end of the day. It's a cool job, but it's a job, and you shouldn't kill yourself for any job.

You probably think it's easy for me to say this from the other side of the divide, but it's not. I want to say all that running, all those nights away from my wife, was worth it...

...I'm just not sure if I knew then what I know now that I would have said to move forward, given the risks and the returns.

FIVE YEARS

Will you still be here in five years?

I've been doing this a whole long time, and when people ask how to build a network, especially with established pros, it seems like the one question you have to answer is that.

"Will you be here in five years?"

Because if the answer is no, that is a lot of time investment into somebody who will abandon the industry when the going gets tough.

Notice, I'm not saying you have to be the biggest name or make a living or anything like that. I'm just asking if you will still be hustling away in five years, putting out books and trying to make it happen.

If not, then bringing you into my network is probably not worth it because I have a banging network. It totally slaps, which means I am very protective of it.

If you're nice, we can still be friends, but I'm not going to bring you into my creator network. I'm not going to the mattresses for you.

But we can still get soup and talk about movies.

And those are two different things. Friendship and network are TWO DIFFERENT THINGS.

I will say it again. Being my friend and being in my network are TWO DIFFERENT THINGS.

Yes, being in my network generally means we're friends, but the reverse is NOT true. I have many friends I'm not going to the mattresses for in this industry and some people in my network who I keep at arm's length.

If you want to be in somebody's network, here's the thing.

Pros are looking for people who resonate on the same level of crazy as they do and can deliver on that level of crazy.

Sometimes people think that's mercenary, but I don't think so. Many people are coming up and want to use pros to get a leg up and then have no follow through.

Being in my network means I will recommend you for work and recommend your work to people.

Before I go out of my way to help somebody, my question is always, "Are they going to abandon my audience if I promote them?", or "Are they just going to run away and all the advice I gave them will be useless?"

It takes a lot of energy to build a new relationship, and frankly, the easiest way for me to know if we'll click is if I think you share the same kind of crazy as me, and the best way to know that is if I think you'll be around for the long haul.

Because, if so, then we are kin. Even if I hate your politics, or even you personally, we are kin on some level because you and I share the same passion and drive to bring stories into the world.

I say five years because if you can make it through five years of crap and muck and come out on the other side still wanting to do this work, nothing can stop you.

And do you know the best way to show you're going to be around for five years?

1. MAKE GOOD BOOKS

Let me tell you, the easiest way for me to know you aren't going to make it far is if you show me a bad book. We all have crappy books, but they are in desks somewhere, gathering dust.

If you show me something wonky, I know you aren't ready to be in my network. We might be good friends, but you aren't joining my network until your eye and taste are both impeccable and you can deliver on your ideas with excellent books.

2. BE NICE AND GRACIOUS

I'm not going to recommend you unless you are nice and gracious, along with talented.

3. HIT YOUR DEADLINES

I won't recommend you if you are late with your deadlines. The old rule was that you had to be any two of these: be talented, be good, and/or be on time. Any two of those might have been enough to make a career in the old days, but I expect you to have all three.

4. FOSTER POSITIVITY

This is just my thing, but I want to know if you can interact with your audience in a positive and healthy way. Many creators can't or won't do that.

All those things are how I know if you'll be around for five years or not and the trip-ups that would stop me from adding you to my network.

I want to mention again that FRIENDSHIP and NETWORK are two different things. You can be in neither, either, or both, but they are DIFFERENT.

Finally, you are much better served by making friends with people on the come-up and growing with them because they are the best network. The people you went through the trenches with are the ones who will stick their necks out for you the most.

MARKETING MISTAKE

People sometimes ask me what the #1 mistake people make when it comes to marketing, and to me, there is a clear winner.

They spend WAY too much time worried about people that don't resonate with their message.

People are so focused on the bad comments (me often included) that they forget what it's about...

...finding the few people that DO resonate with their message.

For every 100 people you talk to, you'll be lucky to find 1 that does. It's usually more like 1 in 1,000 who get what you're trying to do.

All the marketing, advertising, showing up to shows when all you want to do is veg out and watch TV...

...all of it is to find the few people who love what you are doing.

Then, you have to gather them together, little by little, over time.

It becomes harder with time because most people will have made up their minds about you, and people's bad attitudes calcify.

But you also get word-of-mouth referrals from people who talk about you with friends and family.

I don't think that you ever become okay with the hatred. You get better at tuning it out and turning it off, but none of that is the point.

You HAVE TO focus on the people who resonate with your message and be willing to handle the people who don't resonate with your message or even actively hate you for no other reason than being born if you ever want to get a big enough audience to truly make a difference at scale with your work.

Or, you have to be willing to say...I don't care about any of that. Even if I only help one person, then it's worth it. You can leave that rat race as long as you're happy where you're at, or you can get okay with it.

The only way I do it now is by focusing squarely on the people who love what I have to say and trying to tune out the other people as best I can.

I am very, very, very liberal with my block button and my unfollow button. Just so liberal with it, and it turned what was a dreadful experience into a pleasant one, for the most part.

SYMPTOMS

A cough could be the result of a cold, the flu, emphysema, tuberculosis, cancer, or any number of things. Taking cough medicine to abate the cough symptom does nothing to abate the underlying disease afflicting your body.

Sure, it will make you feel better in the moment, but the disease will still be festering away in the background, waiting to pop its head back up and attack you again.

The same is true with your business. So often, I hear people say their posts get no engagement, for instance. They try to post different things at different times of the day, but the truth is the engagement issue is a symptom of your audience.

Either you are talking to the wrong audience or too small an audience. However, instead of addressing the root causes of the problem, people spend hours, days, weeks, or sometimes even years fixing the presenting symptom instead of the root cause of their problems.

Worse, they throw money at the symptom instead of the cause, which is throwing money away. You can only get so much engagement from a 100-person audience. Eventually, you will tap out and be unable to grow anymore. Similarly, you can only get so much engagement by talking to the wrong people.

"Cures" are usually not cheap, but they can fix the root cause of your problems. Unfortunately, usually, cures are not sexy or fun. Chemotherapy is much harder and more painful than chugging cough medicine.

However, if you want to send your cancer into remission, cough medicine will do nothing to help you. Only by treating the root cause of our problems can we grow as creators and reach the next level.

DROP THEIR GUARD

Tell me if this has ever happened to you. You're surfing the internet, minding your own business, when suddenly somebody messages you that you haven't talked to in a long time.

It's the worst, right?

And do you know why it's the worst? It's the worst because you know that person wants something from you. You know they are just biding their time until they make their ask. Sometimes, they do it right up front. I love those people because I can immediately ignore them.

But that feeling is horrible, right?

Now imagine it happening ten times a day, which is what it's like to be successful. All day, everyday people message you, asking for things. Sometimes they just come out and say it immediately. Usually, they spring it on you after a couple of minutes.

The more successful you are, the more people come out of the woodwork asking stuff from you as if you are a robot or something.

The more I get these messages, the more I realize that's how I was showing up in other people's life for a long time, too. Whenever I needed something, I would show up and then disappear into the ether. I remember the day I realized I was doing it...not a fun day.

It's a horrible day when you realize you are everything you hate about the world. However, from that day, I vowed to be different. I would not show up just when I needed something. I would check in on people when I wasn't launching books, and vowed not to show up in people's lives just to drain their energy.

And that is the secret to get people to put down their guard. You come to them like they are a human. You treat them like a human. You take an interest in their lives...a genuine interest. Not just about the great stuff but also about the mundane stuff.

This doesn't just go for successful people, either. This goes for everybody. Nothing makes me happier than when fans reply to my emails and let me into their lives. They are all so interesting, and the only reason I know anything about them is because I asked.

The real secret is this, though...you have to care. You can't pretend to care. That doesn't work. You have to want to help, provide something valuable, and then care about the outcome.

If you want to see this in action, message five people you haven't talked to in a long time, out of the blue, and check in on them. It will feel weird at first, but at the end, when you say, well, great talking to you, there is almost an air bubble that gets popped and a deep sigh of relief that is almost palpable.

The more you do this, the more you will be the kind of person who asks about people's lives in a meaningful way.

Those are the people who get ahead because they are the ones people want to help.

Most people come to me complaining they aren't making any money, and I ask them how they show up for their fans and the people around them. Oh man, you do not want to be around when the veil comes crashing down around them.

We all have issues and need money eventually, and there's nothing wrong with asking when you do, but you have to come to grips with the fact that if you are always asking and never giving, then people will always have their guard up around you. Life will be hard, and you will likely not get much traction because nobody wants to help a taker.

They want to help a giver.

WHY EVEN TRY?

In the face of so much destruction, chaos, and zealots pulling us inextricably back to the past, why even try to do anything?

If I've learned anything in this life, it's that the universe defaults to entropy.

It doesn't want to move forward. Even when it's forced to advance in fits and sparks, it still tries to lurch back to where it was comfortable.

It welcomes destruction because destruction helps it return to its preferred state.

If everything somebody cares about is destroyed, they will no longer fight entropy, and the universe will win.

The opposite of destruction is creation. It is a powerful force, but unfortunately, creation takes 100x the effort of destruction.

Destruction is easy.

It takes almost no effort to destroy. Hours spent building something beautiful can be ripped apart in minutes.

Creation, though...that takes effort. It takes staring into the abyss and telling it you won't go away.

It takes fighting against entropy and putting something new into the world.

It might be a small thing to you, but simply creating something, even a very little thing, shows the universe that it can go screw itself.

It shows other people that you don't care how bad things are; they should keep trying to make things better, even if only in fits and sparks.

And in that creation, embedded into the very foundation of it, is a tiny fount of hope.

It's small, almost imperceptible, but it's there in everything that has ever been created.

Because if you can put something into the world, maybe so can somebody else, and if enough people do that, it will fight against the entropy pulling us down into destruction and chaos.

Everybody needs hope right now. Every person with a shred of empathy believes deep down that hope is fading if it's not already lost.

When that hope is lost, the universe has won. Maybe not today or tomorrow, but eventually, entropy will win.

But watching people create things, even if it's the littlest, dumbest thing ever, is its own form of rebellion.

Creating things is the essence of punk.

It's why artists have always been equally lauded and persecuted. It's why in authoritarian regimes, they tear down the art first.

Dictators HATE hope.

They know that if they can destroy hope, then all that they have left is acquiescence.

By showing them you can still create, you show that you have fight left in you, that they have not won.

Even if you do not make political art, simply making art is political because it gives hope to the masses, and that hope is how they continue the fight.

Is this too much to put on an artist? Absolutely.

Is it pretentious to say that creating art can save the world? Probably, at least a bit.

But that doesn't make it any less true...

...and even if it is not true, it is a lie that hurts nobody and breeds hope.

If I am going to lie to myself, then at least let it be a good lie.

LIFE-CHANGING THINGS

Big, life-changing things do not happen quickly, and they don't happen often.

They are a collection of a thousand meetings that don't work out to come up with one thing that does.

It's a hundred dates that sucked to find the person you will spend the rest of your life with.

It's a thousand lost stories to find the one that resonates with people.

But the thing is, you don't need that many.

You only need one spouse, for most people. You only need one business partner, if that. You only need one project to turn your career around.

Even with all my work, I've only worked with a handful of artists on my personal stuff in my career. I've only hired a few editors and even fewer proofreaders.

You don't need many collaborators to change the world, but finding those collaborators is a lifelong pursuit.

Ichabod Jones took nearly a decade to get off the ground and find an audience. The Godsverse Chronicles took five years, and I'm still trying to stand it up properly with every passing day.

Cthulhu is Hard to Spell was eight years of trying to figure things out, launching, failing, launching again, and learning what people wanted.

Meanwhile, I have made dozens of projects that didn't resonate like those. For every Cthulhu, there are a dozen *Invasion*s and *The Marked Ones.* Good projects that didn't hook enough people and fizzled.

I have been creating courses and teaching about launching Kickstarters since 2011. It took until 2020 to find Monica Leonelle, another year before we launched Get Your Book Selling on Kickstarter, and another six months to launch the Accelerator, which just raised $35,000 in one launch.

There were THOUSANDS of hours of work behind the scenes over the better part of a decade to make that one look easy. It was only all our failures that made that one a success.

Ichabod was years of building, building, building, at every show, on every interview, and pushing it up a hill before it finally found an audience. Only having *Katrina Hates the Dead* and then *Pixie Dust* allowed that series enough time to find its fandom.

We just signed two deals for books we've been working on for four years, and we have other deals we can't even talk about that have been going on for much longer.

If you are worried that everything seems to be taking forever or falling apart, guess what?

That's part of it. That's almost all of it.

Ideas are brittle.

They crumble in your hands most of the time and then break apart under the slightest pressure at other times.

It's the very rare idea that lasts for a long time and the even rarer one that lets you build a lasting career.

I have done SO much stuff you don't even know about to build the foundations I now stand on, and still, almost everything crumbles apart under the slightest pressure put on it.

That is why people are a 10-year overnight sensation because it takes that long maneuvering behind the scenes to make something work, and even then, it is fragile.

It is why people go back to the well on remakes and sequels because it's so rare to find something that resonates and that has the ability to push through the noise.

When you look back at your career, if you have a few things that lasted long term, that's an epic accomplishment.

That's the game. Having ideas, trying to put them together, and having them fall apart for one reason or another.

Meeting people and trying to collaborate only not to have it mesh at that moment or ever.

It's all of it.

I have walked up to a hundred plates and taken my shot, only to strike out. I still feel like I haven't hit a home run yet, but I can get on base and make it around the bases, sloppy as it is.

That's my career as a grinder.

If you are having a bunch of meetings that fall apart, then I commend you because that's the work.

If you're doing things that don't resonate, congratulations, because that's the work, too.

If you are building something, and it's shaky and wobbly, then guess what? That's also the work.

It's nearly impossible to stand anything up in the long run. I have worked on hundreds, maybe thousands of projects, and they almost all evaporated into the ether.

Some lasted long enough to make back their investment, but others didn't. Some won't come out for a long time, and many you'll never see.

And some of those things that barely got off the ground...they are some people's favorite books I've ever made. People still ask me about *Paradise* and how *Sorry for Existing* changed their lives.

I have been told that *Worst Thing in the Universe* is somebody's favorite book enough times to wonder if every person who read it loved it so much that it became their favorite book because it did not sell enough copies for how revered it is by some people.

These books were failures in the eyes of the publishing community, but they worked for those people, and that's enough too for some projects.

I expect when my career is done, people will talk about *Cthulhu is Hard to Spell, Ichabod Jones: Monster Hunter,* The Godsverse Chronicles, and maybe The Obsidian Spindle Saga as the legacy, maybe my work with Monica as well if it gets popular enough.

That's 3-5 things, and I've written dozens of books and comics, both fiction and non-fiction. I'll write dozens more before the end, and some will resonate with a small group, but I don't think anything will ever break through like those did.

But I've done much more than those books, and some books nobody talks about are people's favorites.

It's just all under the surface, and let me tell you, some of those projects that never got off the ground break my heart.

KEEP THE SPARK

Since March, I have been on 81 podcasts, assuming I have not miscounted. On every one, they ask me how I became a writer, and I've answered a lot of different ways, but the one I keep coming back to is that I never knew that wasn't what you were supposed to do.

When I was young, everybody wanted to be a director, a writer, or an actor.

I just assumed that when I hit 40, everybody would have done that thing. It didn't cross my mind for one second that it wouldn't happen.

I was intimidated, frankly, because there was so much talent around me.

Then, life happened, and I looked back 20 years later and realized that just because you wanted to do something didn't mean that's what happened.

I tell people that the great separator is time and effort.

When you're at the starting line, there are millions of people around you, but as you keep doing work, people fall off until you're one of a few, a select group, that has kept the creative spark.

You have no idea how rare that gift is until you sit back 20 years after high school and think about all the people who wanted to do something creative with their lives and how few ended up doing it.

There are many aspiring creatives, but so few make it to the mountaintop with their spark intact that it's almost a miracle it ever happens.

I'm not saying they aren't happy. Many of my friends who stopped doing creative work are happy but aren't doing the creative thing they set out to do when we were wee babies.

They aren't doing the thing that intimidated me about them for so long.

People more talented than you will fall away. People who boast more will go away. People you think are guaranteed to win will go off and do something else. Hotshot creators will burn bright, burn fast, and burn away. I've seen it all while I've been slowly doing the work day after day.

My work has never been perfect. Far from it, but I've learned from it every step of the way and kept going. Showing up and making the best work you're capable of is the secret to the whole game. It's not one or the other. Making one great product doesn't give you a career. Showing up without making something doesn't make a career. Showing up and doing great work consistently makes a career, especially if you can keep showing it to more and more people.

At the end of the day, you will be alone on a mountain, and you'll look around at other mountains and see the other people who climbed the summit, and you will bond with them instantly because they were the survivors.

In this work, most of it is about surviving with the creative spark still inside you, protecting it fiercely, and outlasting other people.

MONEY IN COMICS

Alright. Here it is, the magic, secret sauce for making money in comics.

1. **Make a comic issue for a reasonable price = less than $3,000/issue.** You might need to cut page count, but $2,000 is the real sweet spot.
2. **Make sure your books are no more than 150 pages at the end of the day.** Write arcs or complete stories to those specs. 100-150 is the sweet spot for selling it high and buying it low.
3. **Invest in the production of 2 issues ($4,000).** Expect to spend another $2,000 on printing to print 2,000 books. Selling those books out will net you $10,000 if you sell them at full price.
4. **Now you are in the hole with $6,000.** You need to do some sort of pre-order campaign to raise the funds for those books—Kickstarter, your own site, or however you do it.
5. **With a good campaign, you can expect to raise $1000-$2500 on book one and $1500 to $3000 on book two.** If you do this right, you will either break even on all costs for the first graphic novel or come close.
6. **Now, you have 100-150 pages of art that are completely paid for or close to it.** Next, you run another pre-order campaign for the trade, which will net

you the most money (Since you've built your audience with single issues), AND it will be all profit after you pay print costs. If you can raise $10,000 to print books, you will most likely be able to print 2,000 copies and only need to send out 400-500, giving you 1500 books of pure profit or $30,000 of profit on a $20 trade.

Then, rinse and repeat. I don't care how much you research. That's how you make money in comics. Argue and complain all you want. Try to find another trick. There isn't one. That's how Marvel and DC have done it for years. That's how I do it. It's how it's done.

MESSING UP

A few days ago, my friend said to me, "I'm just so frustrated that when I try, I still screw up."

I smiled at him and said, "Of course you do. That's the whole point."

And it's true.

Doing nothing leads to making no mistakes, but any time you try ANYTHING, you will screw it up, at least a little bit. Even the most beautiful art in the world is riddled with mistakes, false starts, and disappointment.

The only way you can get anywhere good is by trying, and trying, by definition, means you will fail. I fail ALL the time. I have never had a book outline that didn't get blown up while I was writing the book, and I've never had a book that I sent to the editor thinking it was perfect.

More importantly, my editor has never given me back a book saying there were no corrections to be made. Every artist I've ever worked with has changed panel descriptions to fit the story, and I've had to rewrite every script I've sent out once I saw the final panels.

Yes, the final product is wonderful, but it's not the exact thing I set out to make. It never will be because there will be mistakes and corrections along the way.

Wow, thinking about that makes me realize how many mistakes I make on a regular basis. My goal is not to make the same mistake twice, or barring that three times, or barring--well, you get the picture.

There are a million mistakes folded into life because there are a million things you have to try if you want to grow.

Mistakes are baked into the cake of trying, even when you know what you're doing. When you don't know what you're doing, there will be even more mistakes because you're still trying to figure it out.

I'm not saying mistakes are fun. They always make you feel bad in the moment, but you should celebrate them because mistakes mean you are trying, and trying means you are growing. On the other side of growth is success, maybe not today or tomorrow, but eventually, and that's the goal after all, isn't it?

ANYTHING

It's not essential to win the game today. Give yourself a break.

You don't have to do it all.

Just do something.

Anything.

MOVING THE NEEDLE

Q: What advice have you been given about Kickstarter/Convention/Online sales that actually moved the needle and didn't cost a fortune?

A: Working and networking with other creators to build your audience is the cheapest and easiest thing to do. Form a little working group and put your first issue or first trade into a bundle with theirs. Give it away for free or cheap, and share it around with all of you. That should be good for a couple hundred to a thousand new email leads, and social media follows.

Run giveaways with cool packs targeted to a specific audience who you think will like your books, or join with other people to get more marketing muscle behind it. Group giveaways, where you can build your social media and email list are how I started my marketing company years ago.

Get your pitch down to 30 seconds for each book, and create sales sequences for in-person and email automation sequences to turn a new person into a fan. What people are looking for in each series is different, so you have to walk them through the process for each universe.

Pare down your universes so you only have a couple of main things you are selling, and make sure that each of those things has a high likelihood of leading to a sale. People are often very focused on selling ALL things, but you should be doubling down on your most profitable products. If you don't have one that is a runaway hit, you need to do more creating until you come up with at least one that is a smash hit.

Learn how to overcome objections better. This is one of the easiest things to learn. People learn their pitch, but they don't tailor it to people to get the best result, and they don't have a way to overcome the most common objections to their work.

Learn your audience better. Almost nobody knows their audience well enough to target properly or has the right words to get the right people to notice and buy their work.

Develop a cohesive brand where the RIGHT person will look at it and immediately love it, or at least be drawn to it. People should be able to look at your logo and know, "that's the person who does x".

You can also start going on podcasts and other comic-related shows, which takes time to research and go on, but costs no money. However, it usually does mean training yourself to be a magnet for your perfect fans so that they will get excited about your work when they hear your work. You have to draw excitement for your work.

Those are the things I usually find that people AREN'T doing but can be doing, both in-person and online, which are cheap, cheap, cheap to do.

You can network with other people. You can do group giveaways with people as often as possible, and if you lead it, you might even be able to get free entry or maybe even make money on it if you're really good.

Learning your audience is as easy as reaching out to them and asking questions about them to unearth where to find more people like them.

Rebranding might take a couple of hundred dollars, but most companies have brands that have no personality and could do with a change to get people excited about it. Changing your brand to speak to your audience better is an easy way to increase sales. Once your brand resonates with the right people, more people will find you without having to lift a finger.

Bookfunnel, Prolific Works, KingSumo, Rafflecopter, StoryOrigin, and Facebook messenger have meant everything to my growth, along with a powerful network.

And there is one thing.

Change of attitude.

If you hate doing marketing and networking, it will show with people 100% of the time, and they will be turned off. So, you have to change your mindset to say, "I GET to reach out to people", instead of feeling it is a burden or frustration. That is also free.

MENTAL HEALTH DAYS

Yesterday was a bad mental health day.

You are allowed bad mental health days.

You shouldn't feel guilty for good mental health days, either.

This is a time of incredible change, and neither your body nor your mind are used to moving so fast.

Today was a bad mental health day, but hopefully, tomorrow will be better.

LOOK TO THE PAST

I am reminded this morning of the fact that while many people look forward to the next project, few look backward at the assets they already have.

Relaunching old projects, combining old projects in new ways, repackaging long-dead projects, and generally looking back to your backlist is a great way to make some money while you are flailing around in the dark to find any creative spark.

I guarantee there are still more people out there who haven't bought your old stuff, no matter how well it sold.

We are so quick to fall in love with the new that we forget how much love and care is in our past.

I have recovered and relaunched so many books in my life, revitalizing them and injecting much-needed cash into my business.

It's true that nothing sells your old books like a new one, but equally true is that if you don't have the energy to make something new, you can do much with what you've already made.

DO NOT ASSUME

If you find somebody that resonates on your frequency of weirdness, DO NOT assume you will ever see them again.

Make and maintain that connection starting now.

Finding those people is magic, and whether they are creators or fans, do not assume you can "catch them at the next one".

If the pandemic has taught me anything, it's that there might never be a next one.

If you make a connection with one awesome person a month for the next five years, that's 60 people. That's an awesome network of fellow weirdos. If you can do it once a week, you've got over 200. Once a day for five years, and that's over 1800 people.

Five years may seem like forever, but it's the blink of an eye in a career. It really is.

I am very blessed to have found so many people who resonate with my frequency, but I have also done the hard work of connecting with them, maintaining that connection, and cultivating it.

BE A CONNECTOR

Last weekend, I had trouble sleeping before the final day of ALT FCD, the show I ran with my friend Neo Edmund to replace a little piece of what the comics community lost with the postponement of Free Comic Book Day.

It's not uncommon for me to have insomnia on the night of a big show.

As I tried to tire my brain out, I thought about connections and how being a connector is the easiest way to level up quickly and grow your career.

When I was starting out, searching for somebody to take me seriously, I found a group of humans living in LA who loved comics and worked in entertainment through a group called Comic Book Sunday. I did and still do, think they were the coolest people on the planet.

Once a month, a bunch of people would meet in a studio, house, or backyard somewhere in LA, and talk about comics.

When I was trying to be taken seriously, everybody else in the world either laughed or scoffed, but they all took me seriously and welcomed me into their little club.

From there, I connected with so many people I still consider dear friends today, and I was just in awe of how the organizers brought so many people together.

I cannot count the number of amazing connections I made from that group and how it helped me level up about 100 times over, and probably more than that.

I'm still reaping the benefits of that group to this day.

Not only does Neo Edmund, the co-founder of ALT FCD, have a direct connection to CBS being one of the founders, but at least a half dozen speakers have direct lines from that group to ALT FCD as well.

When Neo and I became friends, I asked him how the heck he was able to do it, and he said something along the lines of "we just all loved comics and wanted to meet up to talk about it, and then a few people turned into a few dozen people turned into a few hundred people".

I thought it was magic, but he talked about it so plainly that it made complete sense at the same time. He even made it seem easy and logical.

Cut to a few years later, and I was not getting very far in my career in comics, movies, or anywhere, really. I had done a couple of Kickstarters, exhibiting at shows, and I was meeting people, but I was flatlining.

I wanted guidance from successful creators about how they built their careers, but nobody has an hour to spend at a con yapping at some nobody.

I realized, though, that if I could connect somebody to an audience, then I could use that audience to entice them...

...and my podcast was born.

I interviewed dozens of creators, asked them all about how they built their careers, facilitated deep and meaningful conversations, and then, when it was done, introduced them to my audience.

I learned then that you could punch way out of your league when booking guests. I booked Paul Jenkins a couple of months in when I had NO BUSINESS interviewing somebody of his legendary caliber.

I realized, though, that you didn't even need a big audience. You just needed to be memorable, make a real connection, and build a bridge.

And I did it again and again because everybody wanted to reach an audience, and they wanted to feel heard.

Our need for connection runs so deep that if you can facilitate that conversation and deliver an amazing experience for people, they will open up to you.

If you can make a connection, then you're somebody special. If you are the pivotal cog, you become nearly irreplaceable.

I took every piece of advice they gave, implemented as much as possible, and eventually broke through myself.

I learned from those first interviews how to interview creators well and bring something new into the world that people would enjoy and that the guest would enjoy. The first one wasn't perfect...they are still never perfect...but I've gotten so much better through practice.

I knew that if the guests were happy, if they felt the conversation had merit, and they left with a smile, I had a chance to connect with them outside the show and make a friendship. I didn't care if that friendship led anywhere. I just wanted to be connected to more creatives I respected in a deep and meaningful way.

That podcast grew and evolved into The Complete Creative brand, which generated half of my revenue for years.

Meanwhile, roughly at the same time as I started the podcast, I was still barely inching forward as a creator.

I had a couple of publishing deals, but none worked out, and I was struggling to get my own company off the ground.

I had no idea how to get to the next level, but I had a group of other creators I admired and wanted to work on something with them.

I wanted to get into anthologies, but nobody was hiring me for them, so I took matters into my own hands. As I had realized much earlier, if nobody else wants to take a chance on you, you can do it yourself.

So, that's what I did.

I learned long ago that people LOVE being a part of something but hate organizing anything, so if you can organize something and do it well, people will willingly join.

But there was something else I learned all the way back in those CBS days.

People join something, and they WANT to tell other people about it when they're having fun. When people are making connections, leveling up, and enjoying each other, word spreads by itself.

I decided that it wasn't enough to make something amazing with friends.

It has to be phenomenal; yes, that's the standard for making anything, but more than that, it has to be fun. It has to be so much fun that people can't help but share it.

The creators have to love each other so much and their stories so much that they are overflowing with joy to share them.

They had to get so much out of it, whether that was friendships, other work, rising to the next level, or money, that they would never forget it.

In fact, they needed to get ALL of that and more.

So, I made sure that not only did people submit to an awesome anthology and they were proud of the final product, but that they had a good experience along the way and that they connected with each other on a real level. That they found each other and made a little tribe together, that they laughed and mingled together, and that they developed a real connection through the book.

If I could do that, then the book would transcend to be more than the sum of its pages and make a real impact on my career and the world.

The result of that was *Monsters and Other Scary Shit,* and if you don't know, that book made my career.

Yes, I was doing okay before, but that book rocketed me up 100+ levels practically overnight.

The book was amazing, yes, but there are many amazing books on Kickstarter, and anthologies that I've now been part of, that don't make $27,000 on Kickstarter; that people don't talk about years later.

I made *Cthulhu is Hard to Spell* from that book and kept the "party going". At each step, I remembered what I learned back in CBS. That book made $39,000 on Kickstarter and launched me up another 100 levels.

If you can connect people and facilitate a good time doing it, word will spread.

But I learned something else.

CBS, at its peak, wasn't huge. It had a few hundred people, maybe a thousand, at its peak, which isn't big for a group.

But they were the RIGHT people.

They were people who were influential and who could move the needle in real, measurable ways. They were producers, directors, editors, writers, and more who were working in the industry, looking for a place to connect.

CBS gave them that; a place where they could stop thinking about work and geek out about the things they loved, with people who they loved seeing, talk about comics, and have a beer.

You didn't need that many people, I realized, to move the needle in a real way. You just needed the right people to connect them, to facilitate joy in them, to get them excited, and then, the rest kind of does itself.

It's more complex than that because it's a living, breathing organism, and you can't just bottle it, but a few dozen of the right people can move mountains.

Cut to 2020; the world ends as we know it.

Everything is canceled.

People need something.

People need connection.

And I know just what to do.

I've been researching virtual summits and virtual conventions for a couple of years...

...all I needed was a couple dozen of the right people to test one, see if it worked, and facilitate some joy for them.

I bought a domain and made a Facebook post, just like I did with my first anthology...

...just a domain and a Facebook post...

...that's all it took.

I asked who would be available to go live for a bit, created a little website, and figured out how to make the creators involved happy...

...because if they were happy...if they could connect with each other, and the audience...

...then maybe I could bottle magic again.

I ran that first event and got a lot of fantastic feedback from the creators, but really...

...I don't think I did much.

I facilitated them getting in front of new people...

...I facilitated them meeting each other...

...and I made sure they looked great doing it, so they could be the best version of themselves.

This is important because I've spent hundreds of thousands of dollars running tests, making things, and trying to build myself up little by little...

...but the most successful things I've ever done...

...the things that moved the needle...

...cost the least.

They were time investments, sure, but *Monsters and Other Scary Shit*, before that Kickstarter ran, cost me $600 to make a cover.

The rest was all time and relying on the investments I had made in RELATIONSHIPS and CONNECTIONS.

That podcast cost me $100 to buy a high-quality microphone and another $200 max to build the website and get the hosting service set, leading to incalculable ROI.

These virtual conferences...

...in total, it cost me around $200 to run all three.

I invested A LOT into relationship costs...

...and connection costs.

With each step along the way, I built out prototypes and proof of concepts and started with something manageable.

I invested thousands of hours of my own time in building out the processes...

...but the investment of capital...

...it's was next to nothing...

The capital investment is small because I invest in relationships and connections all the time.

I invest in learning new processes and going places nobody else even thinks about so that when an opportunity presents itself, I can pounce on it.

My goal, which I learned back in 2010, is to find the right people, connect with them, help them connect with each other, and facilitate joy...

...and not to expect anything in return, but to hope for a good friendship out of it...

...which doesn't cost anything, but it costs everything at the same time.

It's not something you need a huge budget to do. It costs you something else, though.

It costs you completely changing how you think about everything, value time, and think about the people in your life, though...

...but as for money...nah...you don't need much of that to make a real difference in your life.

I should note that I invest heavily in making my own projects, making them the best they can be, and my exacting standards for my own work mean that when I make good connections and they see my work, they take it seriously. You don't want to blow your shot. You don't want to get somebody to your show or give them a book after you've worked so hard for them to notice you and then blow it with a crappy product.

Making great work takes time, effort, energy, and money. I spent a LOT of my time at the beginning of my career making things until I was confident that I could make something remarkable again and again. That's essential

100% for SURE it is.

And you can't leverage those connections until you can make something great consistently...and I mean great to the point people stop and marvel at it...

...but the stuff that moved the needle for me and brought me to the next level never cost a lot...except it cost everything. Suppose you're at the point in your career where you're CONFIDENT you are making something awesome, and you're not getting the recognition you think you deserve. In that case, being the fulcrum by which people connect to each other is a valuable position, and it's much easier to start doing it than you think.

Being a connector, a nexus by which people can circle around, and provide value through those connections, is the cheapest and most valuable way to build a career and propel yourself forward.

If my career is a model for nothing, it is a model for that, and it's imminently replicable as long as you're willing to put in the time and the work. This isn't something that pays off immediately, but it pays off in dividends when you do it right.

THANKS, AND NO

You are not obligated to say yes. Every yes is a new obligation, and it fractures you further and further until nothing is left for you. FOMO is a powerful concept, and I know the desire to say yes to everything, so you don't piss people off or lose opportunities.

However, at some point, there is no more of yourself to give. You have overextended every bit of yourself; the more you give, the more people will take.

I work with a lot of people who want to say no because they are being crushed under their obligations but don't know how to say no.

I'll tell you now, simpler is better. You are not obligated to tell somebody why you are saying no.

You can politely say "thanks, and no."

Users will not like it because there's nothing to manipulate in three words. They are not jerks for asking, but they are jerks for pressuring you after you said no.

Manipulators will keep trying to pressure you, and if they do, then you were right to say no.

If they let it go and say, "thanks for considering it, " you made the right decision.

Your job is to stay underleveraged so that when something GREAT comes along that is a full-body "HECK YES," you have the time for it.

Do not justify your decision, or make it conditional, because then people will try to meet the conditions and coerce you into saying yes. If you tell somebody you can't do it because of x or y reason, you have left it open for them to say, "well, can we revisit it later?" or, "So if one of those things cancels, can I book you?"

That's why a simple, "thanks, and no", is the best response.

If they come back and say, "you really should do it because of x", you can say, "I appreciate that, and no."

Don't say, "but no", because "but" seems both negative and conditional.

A simple, "Thanks, and no," should be all you need to say to somebody who respects your boundaries.

If they don't respect your boundaries, they will try to weasel around anything else you say to guilt you into doing it, so don't give them a chance.

It's quite empowering to leave it at three words.

BROKEN

If you make something that is objectively good, defined by the fact that it is of a high quality that can be seen by an array of people even if it's not their cup of tea, then there is a mathematical certainty that there is an audience for that work.

The problems arise when:

- The audience of potential true fans is not big enough to be found easily, meaning you will have to spend a long time, significant funds, and a lot of effort to find them.
- The potential audience might be too small to justify a product at the price point you are charging. It's hard to sell a $5 product to a 100-person audience.
- You aren't releasing products at the frequency necessary to succeed with the potential audience.
- The runway you have given yourself isn't long enough to find success, and you run out of money.
- You do not have enough material to rise above the noise and be found by people who are looking for you.
- You are not finding new people to add to your ecosystem on a regular basis.

- You aren't finding enough people on a regular basis to add to your ecosystem. This is DIFFERENT from the above.
- You do not have an effective process to show those people why they should care about you.
- You are looking in the wrong places.
- You are talking to the wrong people.
- You are building the wrong thing for the people you want to serve.
- Your voice is not honed to deliver a consistent experience to the readers you are attracting to tell them your work is right for them.
- You don't spend enough time connecting to those people you attract.
- You simply haven't been doing it for long enough to catch on.

This assumes that a wide swath of people can look at your work and say that it is good (and mean it), even if they cannot articulate why or even if it is not their jam. I'm not talking about people who love you too much not to lie to you. I'm talking about new people who don't like you enough to lie to you.

The question is, where is your problem? Is it in making objectively good products, or is it in one of the areas above?

I don't know the answer, but those are the major areas I see consistently when it comes to creative folks. Audit every piece of that equation and make sure you are solid at every piece because I guarantee you have a fault somewhere in that chain. It's essential to be objective with this, too. Lying only hurts yourself. If you don't know the answer to one of these questions, do some digging. *I don't know* is not an appropriate answer, and almost always, if you don't know, the answer is probably you need to work on that problem with focused intention.

Once you are making a good product, consistently, for the right people, in the right place, and working to find new people consistently...then you WILL have growth. If you're not getting it, something's broken, and only one possible part of it is that your work isn't very good. More importantly, when something is broken, you don't throw it out. You work to repair it, and almost nothing is beyond repair with a little elbow grease.

"ARE YOU TRYING TO INSULT ME?"

I have been giving mental exercises to artists for a while in private conversations when they talk about how they don't like their own work.

It's been really helpful for them, so I thought I would share it publicly. After all, feeling inadequate is a very common feeling amongst creatives and quite #relatable.

When I hear that, though, I respond with, "what an insulting thing to say to me."

That immediately jolts them to attention. After all, they are down on themselves, right? How could it be about me?

"I like your work," I continue. "And if you're saying it's bad, then you are saying I have bad taste. Is it your intention to insult me like that? Because, if not, then your work can't objectively suck because if it sucked, I would be enjoying sucky work, and I am very sure my taste doesn't suck."

I've used this trick on myself countless times in my own life. Whenever I get down on my work, I ask myself, "Do I think the people who enjoy my work have bad taste?"

Since I love my fans, the last thing I want to do is insult them, so I always say no, which means that my work can't suck, otherwise, my fans would be buying garbage, and I don't think they would do that.

- **Can a book be niche?** Sure.
- **Could you have to work to increase your audience?** Always.
- **Does your art style need more mass-market appeal?** Maybe.
- **Can you always improve your art?** Of course.
- **Does that mean every piece you make is a masterpiece?** No.

I'm not saying the process can't suck or your work doesn't live up to expectations when you're done, but the moment somebody comes to me and says, "I really liked that", I have to step back and say, "This work might not be doing what I want it to do, but can't possibly suck because somebody enjoyed it and I don't want to insult their intelligence or taste."

Otherwise, I'm insulting my audience and telling them they have bad taste, and I would never want to do that.

BORING

I run what is, at its core, a boring company.

I don't do variant covers. I don't have a lot of art prints. I don't do a lot of merch.

My books sometimes come with back matter content, but it is all complete before I launch a Kickstarter.

My stretch goals are easily fulfilled digital rewards from other creators.

I make beautiful books, that is true, and they are expertly crafted, but the process itself is quite boring.

However, that boring company keeps putting out books, delivering on time, or before the expected date, without many moving pieces.

Other companies might look sexier or raise more money, but I just keep sitting here, delivering a one-man shop with freelancers and feeding my audience what they want.

I have now done that for five years. Find an audience, feed them new work consistently, and make books of such high quality that people notice.

And not overextending myself.

Meanwhile, I watch the majority of creators I know overextend themselves with t-shirts, merch, and other stuff before they are ready.

I watch them add 40+ pages to their book on a whim because they think it will be cool and then delay a campaign fulfillment by a year, breaking the trust they have with their audience.

Or, worst of all, delivering something that looks jank, unprofessional, or unimpressive, completely turning people off from becoming repeat buyers.

Everything I do is worked out and managed at least a year in advance.

It is very boring but predictable. The differentiating factor is that the books will be of higher quality than anything else on the market, and they will be delivered both expediently and of the same quality every time.

The books themselves are amazing, of course, but the process is simple, repeatable, and boring.

Every time it is the same, meaning when I promise something, I can deliver it.

Yes, perhaps I should have expanded some years ago. Yes, perhaps I have shot myself in the foot at certain times because I haven't chased a big deal and thrown my company into peril.

However, everything I've done can be handled exquisitely by a single person or with the strategic hiring of freelancers.

Very boring. No surprises. No frills. Just beautiful books. No heartstrings tugging me in a direction that my workload can't handle.

And I wish every creator had a boring company built on solid foundations instead of the chaotic messes I find at every turn.

ANOINTED

There is a choice you have to make in your career.

Do things the "right" way, and hope somebody anoints you from above and brings you up to their level...

...or figure out how to anoint yourself and pull yourself up to the next level.

Gatekeepers don't want you to anoint yourself, so they will fill your head with tales about how people who anoint themselves are cocky, arrogant, or breaking everything.

But that is because we don't wait for them to tell us we're good enough.

We don't wait for them to tell us we're ready.

Because we know they never will. They will never anoint you. They will anoint their chosen ones, but they will never anoint you.

If you wait for them, you'll be waiting a long time. I know people who have been waiting for the agent for a decade.

I know people who've had their agent for a decade and still haven't gone out with a project.

I know people who've been going out with projects for a decade and never sold any of them.

Russell Nohelty

They've been waiting to be anointed.

Meanwhile, I've released books, made money, and scraped every day to build my audience...

...and I've anointed myself.

It was hard. It was grueling. Nothing about this was easy...except for me to keep going...

...because there was no other way.

Because I knew they would never anoint me, and if I waited, I would be stuck in the cold, looking in, for the rest of my life. If you anoint yourself, though, you have to work hard. You have to work so hard, and you can't wait. You have to pull yourself up and make it happen.

I know so many people who say they are anointing themselves, but then they sit back and wait. You can't do that. If you're going to anoint yourself, you have to learn how to do it, brick by brick, until you don't need them to pull you up because you've built your own ledge.

DICTUMS

I live my business life by a very simple goal:

That at the end of my career, when all is said and done, those I've worked with will single me out as one of the best collaborators/projects they worked on in their careers.

That means talented but also friendly, cordial, open to notes, kind, on time, etc.

It encompasses everything from conception through the end result, as there can be no weak links in the chain. I can't write a great script and then never pay for art.

I can't write something mediocre and toss it away without a care.

It means every project has to be world-class from end to end.

It's a pretty simple dictum, but it influences everything else in my career.

I used to play golf a lot, and when I played golf, they would say you can have at most three things go through your head before you swing.

If you have any more, you're going to choke. So I choose:

1. **Make every project the best of your collaborator's career.** *(for business)*
2. **Anything you can do that doesn't hurt yourself or other people is fine with me.** *(for personal)*
3. **Treat everyone like a complete, three-dimensional person with hopes, needs, and dreams.** *(for both)*

I can remember those, and they penetrate every other moment of my whole life. We make things complicated, and yes, there are about a million caveats that go into each of those dictums, but at the end of the day, that's what I need running through my head to perform at my best and make sure everybody else is performing at theirs.

PROMOTIONAL CALENDAR

A couple of years ago, I was strict about creating a promotional calendar throughout the year.

Before a year begins, I plot out my big promotions, my big mailing list-building scenarios, and everything else.

Whenever I talk to people about their plans, I always try to get them to make a promotional calendar.

How do you make one?

First, block out your major promotions for the year. If you're planning BIG promotions, like Kickstarters or huge course launches, then you'll want to plan NO MORE than four in a year, generally, one a season.

It doesn't have to be one a season, but for beginners at planning something like this, it's helpful to keep everything in three-month chunks.

Before you start blocking promotions, you will want to make sure what you're planning doesn't have any dead zones.

For instance, launching books in November or December is not very good, especially after Thanksgiving, because ad spend goes up drastically during that time.

Is there a big event happening, like an election or holiday, like Memorial Day, when ad buys will also go up dramatically, and the world will be focused on something else?

If so, knock those off your calendar, or at least that kind of promotion off your calendar. You can, for instance, launch a course in November/December, but a book is not advisable, and a Kickstarter after Halloween is out unless you can deliver before the holidays.

Then, you block, giving at least a month between the DELIVERY of the last product and the launching of the new product.

As you get further into your career and build more clout, you can potentially launch multiple products without delivering on the last one yet, but if you are a newbie, always deliver before you launch.

I like launching in January, June, and September. Then I usually launch in March, too, but end before tax day, and don't usually launch in the fourth quarter at all, so you don't HAVE to follow the once a quarter suggestion. Still, I do recommend launching different types of products if you are going to do them close together.

For instance, I am launching a comic anthology in March and then a trade of a comic in September. I launched a book series in January, and I'll launch another one in June, so I'm spacing out the same kind of books to capture different fans with each promotion and not overload them.

Once you've blocked out the main promotions, you want to block out the main audience-building events. Each big promotion should correspond with AT LEAST one audience-building event.

This is because you'll funnel out a lot of people during the promotion period, and you'll need to build back up again and focus on GIVING your audience something after you asked for something for so long.

I generally schedule at least two audience-building events between campaigns.

I like to schedule the first audience-building event a couple of weeks after my campaign ends and at least a month before the launch of the next campaign.

I like to schedule my second one RIGHT before the next launch and make it more focused on the product I'm about to launch.

Everything else in my promotional calendar falls around those big launches. If I have other anthologies or books to promote or other things I need to promote, they have to slot in and around those big launches, and they will likely only get 1-2 days of promotion max.

The caveat is that if you have two businesses, you can have two promotional calendars. I still don't recommend promoting two things at once, but assuming you have two different audiences and not a lot of overlap on either, then you will have two different promotional calendars.

For instance, The Complete Creative and Wannabe Press are two different companies, so I plan launches for courses close to my book launches because I absolutely have to do so, otherwise, I would never launch any courses.

However, if you have only one company, you will only have one promotional calendar.

PRICE INCREASE

During the course of your career, you will have to raise your rates several times. This is never an easy thing to do, especially if you have a steady stream of customers at your current price tier. However, if you want to maximize your revenue, you will need to make your prices higher eventually.

When considering raising your prices, you should first make a list to justify all your accomplishments since the last time you raised your prices. When you look at all your accomplishments, it should make raising your prices much easier. Usually, we downplay our accomplishments in our own brains, but seeing them written out on paper brings our growth into stark focus.

Here is an example from my own career. When I launched my first big course, *Build a Rabid Fanbase,* I had no experience launching large courses.

For that reason, I set the price $200 below my final price, at $297, when I launched it in January 2018. I was massively undervaluing the course, but I had my reasons.

I did this partially because I wanted to give people a compelling reason to buy (the course would only be that cheap for a limited time), partly to convince people to take a chance on me, and, most importantly, to give myself confidence.

See, even though I was giving people a blueprint based on my success, I wasn't sure the course was worth the price. After all, $297 was the most expensive product I had ever launched, by about $250.

Additionally, I wanted to work out all the bugs and ensure people were satisfied before raising the price. For all those reasons and more, the $297 price point made sense to me.

In the ensuing six months, dozens of people took my course and enjoyed it. Many said it was the best course they had ever taken. Some said it revolutionized their career. My confidence grew as I heard stories of other people's success.

By June 2018, I had built enough confidence to raise the price to $397, still $100 shy of my final target price. It would still be at a discount, but significantly less than before.

I wasn't sure people would buy the course when I raised the price, but I had some compelling reasons to do so.

1. **People had gone through the course and loved it.**
2. **I had witnessed massive transformations in people's lives after taking the course.**

Before I raised the price, I contacted people on my list and told them what I was doing, gave them my reasons, and offered one last opportunity to get in on the lower price.

Then, I raised my price and hoped people would still buy the course at $397. They did.

Luckily, I saw no ill effects of raising my price. People still bought the course at the same frequency as before I raised the price.

Woohoo! I had justified my price increase, and it worked. However, I still wanted to raise the price by $100 more. To do that, I needed even more compelling reasons.

The biggest compelling reason to increase the price of the course came in November 2018 when I became a *USA Today* bestselling author.

Putting that on the front of my name was a huge boost in confidence for myself and my customers. That alone was enough of a reason to justify a price increase.

On top of that, I had been doing book marketing for almost a year at that point, and during that time, I watched my audience, and the audience of my clients grow by tens of thousands using the principles I taught in the course.

I proved my methods throughout the year, using myself as a guinea pig and my customers as social proof. Those two compelling reasons gave me everything I needed to justify a second price increase.

In January 2019, I once again told my audience that I was raising my price and gave them one last opportunity to buy the course for $397.

Before I raised my price, I made sure to add the new justifications on my sales page, including my *USA Today* bestseller title and a lot of testimonials, but then I raised the price without hesitation. I didn't second guess myself because I knew the course was worth it.

I could raise my price so easily because I justified the price increase to myself first and then others. The course itself was mostly the same, but I was a different human, and my methods had proven themselves. The power of the course was exponentially higher than it was at launch, even though the content was the same.

This is what I mean by justifying your price increase. When going to increase your services, the question you should be asking is, "What justified this price increase?"

If you can justify it to yourself, you can also justify it to your customers.

Will all of them buy? No. Some will complain, but if you can justify yourself, you will also be able to discuss your qualifications with new customers.

THE SWITCH

Everybody is a fan of something already. Your goal is to take somebody from being a fan of something else into a fan of your work. One of the most common methods to make this happen is something I call "The Switch", and it's remarkably effective if you do it the right way.

The idea is simple.

If somebody likes X and your work is like X, then a person has a very good chance of also liking your work, which we'll call Y. However, they've had years to build up their love for X, and they have no idea who you are or why they should care about you.

The problem is creators often find people who like X and assume they are ready to like their Y, so they immediately whack them over the head with their Y without giving people who like X a reason why they should care about Y first.

Giving them a reason why is critical for The Switch to work.

The Switch is about taking fans from X to Y, but by way of U, or, more accurately, by liking YOU first. The secret ingredient in The Switch is that potential fans start to like YOU before they like your work. If you can take somebody from liking X to liking YOU, then they will be highly likely to try your Y.

Why is that?

Because you are giving them a REASON why they should like your work which is deeper than just "you like X, so, logically, you will like Y." Instead, you are saying. "Hey, you like me, and you like X. You should try Y because I think you will like it."

When people like you, they are way more likely to try anything you offer them. This is because they've built empathy with you like they would with a friend. Since you know they like X, once they try your work, they will likely love it, too.

The Switch is all about wedging yourself between somebody else's work and your own work and creating empathy between them and you.

Almost everybody misses that middle point and forgets that the easiest way to get people to like your work is to get them to like you. Once you have refined this process, you can start plugging in new people from different existing fandoms and watch your own fanbase soar.

PRACTICE

When you're too tired to think and too upset to move, the one thing that will save you is the practice you put into your work.

The more you have trained yourself to work in every situation, the better you will be able to weather any storm. Often, in my life, it has only been the constant practice that has kept me going.

It allowed me to move on and keep going forward after my dad's death, in the throes of depression, at the heights of anxiety, and in every bad situation.

Those habits I formed in the best times saved me in the worst times.

Will it always work?

No, sometimes I feel so horrible that I can't do even more, but most of the time, I can keep going on muscle memory alone.

The practice doesn't seem worth it until it is needed. Then, it is everything. It's not easy to get there, but it's easy to start. Then, you just have to take it one day at a time.

Studies show it takes at least 66 days to build a habit, but eventually, it will become a habit, and then it becomes easier. It's never easy, but it does become easier.

VALUE OF A SALE

The most important part of any business is the sale.

I don't think that's any revelation there, honestly. However, most people don't truly understand what a sale means for your business. Yes, it does mean revenue NOW, which, you know, we all have bills to pay, but that's not the real value of the sale.

The value of the sale is that once you sell somebody something, you have lowered their defenses, and it becomes much easier to sell to them again. I've seen this in every business I have ever started.

The original sale is brutally and monumentally hard. Getting somebody to part with even one dollar is nearly impossible. However, once you have sold to them, you have an opportunity because you have chipped away at their defenses until they agreed to give you money.

That is not easy.

I very rarely give money to new vendors, and I know most people are like me. They don't have unlimited funds to throw around. Once a new company has "won" my money, it is because I have a deep-seated pain point I think they can solve.

That pain point might be my desire to read an amazing comic, build my email list, learn marketing, or do my taxes. Whatever it is, they have earned the opportunity to win me over with their product.

Most businesses fail when presented with this opportunity, though. Their products are pedestrian or poor. While I rarely ask for a refund, I also put a mental note not to buy from them again.

They have wasted the most valuable part of the sale, which is the returning customer. The one who comes back again and again because they know you are the best and because you take care in your work.

The returning customer is what will make or break your business, honestly. The wider your pool of returning customers, the more of a monetary base you have when launching a new product. If people are eagerly waiting to buy, you could break even or make a profit at launch instead of launching to crickets.

I see people launching to crickets all the time, even established creators, and I know it is because they did not nurture their most precious resource; their existing customers.

Whenever I launch a new product, I first go to my existing customers and ask what they want me to make, and then I go into the marketplace and see if there is a growing market for that product.

In doing that, I could grow my launches from dozens to hundreds to thousands over the year. With each launch, I have a core of customers that will buy my products when they first launch.

Every time I launch a new product line, this same process is true. At first, it's brutally hard because nobody wants to take a chance on somebody new. Over time, they grow to like me, then try one of my products, and then another, and eventually, I have developed a small core of rabid fans.

This was true in comics, novels, marketing, and online courses. Each time it felt equally impossible at first, but then people tried my products and grew to love them. Once they were happy with my products, they started to buy on autopilot.

However, that only happened because I OVERDELIVER on value. No matter the price point, my goal with any product is to blow them away and create the best product they have ever seen at that price point.

Almost no company does this for their customers, at least with any consistency. I can only think of a handful of companies that have earned my repeat business based on the quality and value of the products. That is why most products, and businesses, fail. They focus on the single sale instead of the lifetime value of the customer.

If you build your business on overdelivering, you will always have rabid customers coming back for more. They will talk up your product and drag other people into your ecosystem, making it a virtuous cycle.

That is why it's not good enough to launch a book or a course and expect to have a huge number of sales at first.

At first, you have to develop a baseline of customers who love your work and will eagerly anticipate your next launch. If you keep launching great products and finding new fans, your business will grow.

Remember, though, your customers aren't eagerly anticipating it because they are foolish with their money. They eagerly anticipate it because when they lowered their guard and allowed you into their lives, you didn't take advantage of them like so many others.

Instead, you over-delivered on value, delighted them, and so they became rabid consumers of your work because they know they won't get screwed. That trust is a gift you have to keep earning time and time again.

SUBVERSION

I understand the need for best practices in any field, but it's equally important, probably more important, to learn the hacks around the best practices.

Yes, the best practices are there for a reason, but they are also used by people with more money and experience than you. You will not be able to compete with the big dogs using their methods. Those methods have already been perfected by the big dogs.

The only way to beat the big dogs is to find a way to subvert their methods ethically.

You have to know the methods so well you can recite them in your sleep, but you then need to go deeper and find the ways around those methods which won't get you in legal or ethical trouble. Doing things the way they were done is a great model at the beginning of your career or for learning a new skill, but in studying, you will learn that the way most people do things is broken and time-intensive.

Big companies cannot move nimbly enough to fit through cracks in systems, but you can and should do so at every opportunity. Best practices can help by showing you the consequences of your actions. If you are willing to live with the consequences, then you can make big gains quickly.

Your advantage is being able to turn on a dime and subvert the best practices, exploiting them to your gains whenever possible. There are all sorts of ways to climb the ladder faster, and usually, they come from analyzing the best practices and finding out how to do them in 2 steps instead of 20.

TAPESTRY

Everything you do is a bit of the tapestry you weave.

Every post you make is a piece of thread. No thread is very important on its own, but together they create a beautiful mosaic. It is up to you to weave the thread and tell the story.

You cannot only weave during a launch. You must weave every day, with every post, if you want to build a solid career. You have to show up and sew every single day. Every post somebody sees is another connection to you and builds a bond. The more bonds you make, the stronger your connection and the more complete the tapestry looks to that person.

The more complete they see the tapestry, the more they will connect with you as a person, and the more they will want to support your work. You can't only weave with sales posts, either. You have to show them the complete story of you. Otherwise, they will go away unsatisfied.

I weave my tapestry all day, even though I'm not always launching. At the forefront of my mind is always how to show a more complete version of myself and how I can show up for other people like I would like people to show up for me.

I believe that is one of the secrets to my success. I show up and sew even when there's nothing to be gained from me doing so except making a connection with other humans. I show them the tapestry while I'm weaving, when it's done, and with every step I take along the way.

UNTIL IT DOES

If you keep going, little by little, your work will add up. You won't necessarily feel it every day or even every week, but then one day, it will feel like you leaped forward by a whole year all at once.

Those little things add up to big results given enough time. You have to get out of your own head and understand that you are making progress, even if it doesn't look like it.

TRUST

Trust is not given lightly. It is earned through hard work and consistency. But often, people take for granted people's trust in them.

Trust cannot be taken for granted. Once you have earned somebody's trust, it is incumbent on you to maintain that trust and re-earn it as often as possible. Trust is not necessarily about success. It is about transparency and people's belief that you will try as hard as possible.

Will you always win?

No.

Sometimes you will fail, which sucks, but that does not mean people will lose faith in you. They will lose their trust if they do not believe you did everything you could to be successful and that you aren't doing everything in your power to correct your mistakes.

I've had a lot of mistakes in my career, and every time I've tried to be open and honest about what happened and how I will fix it next time. This is not only how trust is earned but how it is re-earned over and over again. Every time you re-earn somebody's trust, their bond with you becomes stronger.

However, that bond will always be tenuous and fragile. Never take it for granted. It is the best resource you have available to you. If you can accumulate trust at scale and keep that trust with every project, you will never go hungry.

THE ONE THING

What is the one thing you can do today to make it a success?

This is a question I ask myself every morning. It's usually a big thing that will take most of the day, but some days it is quite small.

Asking myself this question allows me to keep focused throughout the day when other things pile on top of my workload.

There are other habits I've formed that become little things I do every day, but they are not my one thing. My one thing is the singular item that will help me leap forward the furthest and the quickest.

Most of the time, it's writing 5,000 words a day or editing 20,000 words of a manuscript. However, sometimes it's recording a course or making a certain amount of money at a show.

The world will pile onto your day, every single day, and try to pull you away from your to-do list, but having a single action item that I know will bring me forward has allowed me to finish more projects than ever because every time I am dragged away, my one thing pulls me back to center again.

DID YOU KNOW?

Did you know you can just...do things?

You don't have to ask permission or anything. Nobody can stop you. They might try to talk you out of it, but they can't stop you from doing it.

You can just...do a thing...

...and then people will know you as a person who did a thing...

...instead of a person who wants to do a thing.

FLOW

I learned a long time ago that it is easier to flow around an obstacle than to try and smash through it.

There is almost always another way around that requires less effort, and if there isn't, then that is probably not the right path anyway.

Not always, but the overwhelming majority of the time.

It is hard enough to flow down even the easiest path. I absolutely refuse to waste my finite resources trying to smash mountains down unnecessarily.

If I did, I would drown in the current.

If I did that, I would have nothing left to expend on the things that matter and the battles truly worth fighting.

Because they do exist, those fights are worth fighting.

Sometimes, there is no choice but to smash against those rocks, and when those moments come, you need all your strength to break through.

If you have to expend all your energy on the fights that don't matter, you will have nothing left for the ones that do.

You might not get your plan A following this advice, but you will progress down the river further than you thought possible and have the energy to take on all the battles you fight along the way.

CONSTRAINTS

Steven Universe and *Game of Thrones* are two shows with very different budgets. *Game of Thrones* costs exponentially more than *Steven Universe.*

Steven Universe is 11 minutes long and animated. *Game of Thrones* is 50 minutes long and live-action.

Steven Universe is created in a studio, while *Game of Thrones* has dozens of locations all over the world.

However, they are both amazing shows. It's just that one takes vastly more resources than the other.

So often, creators try to make *Game of Thrones* on a *Steven Universe* budget.

If you gave the creators of *Game of Thrones* the budget of *Steven Universe*, the show would suck because there would not be enough money to do everything that needs to be done to make *Game of Thrones* into the epic show it became.

That doesn't mean *Steven Universe* sucks, though. Making *Steven Universe* with the budget of *Steven Universe* is perfection.

You need to think differently about your budgetary constraints. If you only have a little bit of money, stop trying to make something that requires 10x more money.

Save that project for later.

Instead, try to make an incredible project with the money and resources you have.

The same is true with skill.

You might be at the beginning of your career and not have much skill. Don't go trying to make an epic book. Instead, try to make an incredible book with the skills and resources you have available to you.

People get this wrong all the time.

It's not about making something grand and epic. It's about making use of the resources you have available to create something amazing and scaling your project to fit your budget.

Once people see that you can make something incredible on a smaller budget, they will be more likely to give you more money for bigger projects.

This is why most filmmakers start with intimate films and then build over time, and how almost every artist grows their skills from shorts and indie books to bigger books over time.

However, if you make a subpar project, people will turn away from you no matter how much money you have available.

Most people try to create the grandest project with a pauper's budget. If you instead tried to fit the project to the budget and scale over time, you would get much further and be happier.

It's a simple flip but powerful nonetheless.

"EVERYONE IS AN AUTHOR"

I am around authors all day, and my brain used to be consumed with thoughts that every human was an author like me. When you think like that, it's hard to get excited about finding new readers because you assume they don't exist.

I mean, who else could there be to buy my books if everybody is an author? Why would they want to buy my books when they're trying to sell their own?

Ever thought like that?

It plagued me for years, but one moment changed all of that for me. I'm used to doing conventions and networking events full of entertainment professionals, but one night I was at a party full of people from my wife's industry, not mine, and it showed me how I was thinking was completely ridiculous.

Because here's the thing.

There were hundreds of people at the party. Yet, not one of them was an author. I'm not saying I talked to every attendee, but I talked to a couple dozen, and all of them said the same thing. They weren't writers. In fact, they were baffled at how I could write things from my imagination. In fact, they told me time and time again they were completely not creative.

Think about that...

I was in a room full of a couple hundred people, and none of them were authors. Almost all of them were readers, though, and most of them told me they read my genres, too, which means a whole bunch of them were my ideal readers.

That opened my eyes. It made me realize that most people in the world weren't authors, which changed everything for me. I was spending all my time stuck in a bubble and believed that because most of my friends were authors, that meant most people in the world must be authors, too.

How often do you think that everybody does what you do? All the time, right? Well, it's not true.

The truth is that most people don't do the things you do. It just seems like it, and because of that, it feels like your market is saturated, but that's because we're all stuck in our own bubbles.

We have to break out of that. There are seven billion people in this world, and most of them don't do what you do. Not even close. It's a huge world out there, and the market isn't flooded. You're stuck in a bubble, just like the rest of us, and you have to pop it.

WORLD-BUILDING HACKS

I am working on my first long book series, and I have learned a couple of tricks through that process that help with keeping the mythology correct.

For example, when you've built up an area with an oppressive amount of mythology, leave it.

Force your characters to an unexplored area of the map, and don't go back to the old area either ever or for a long while until that area of the map has changed.

Then, you can explore the same areas again, completely changed.

It's totally cheating, but audiences eat it up and think you're the greatest world-builder ever instead of just somebody who can't keep their mythology straight or is scared of breaking the universe.

I learned this from video games, except video games make you go back to the starting realm a lot. I prefer to blow up that starting area and force people to use new areas of the map all the time, so I can continue to build the mythology in a new area, which can be completely new mythology than the last area and could even contradict the previous area, based on their views.

It has the ancillary benefit of keeping me interested when I've lost my love for a particular area.

A second tip is that using multiple points of view (POVs) automatically doubles, triples, or exponentially increases the word count and lets you show the same areas from a different character's POV, allowing you to explore the same places or new places with fresh eyes.

Those are the two tricks I've learned for writing long interconnected series. Yes, it's harder to keep the POVs straight, but it's way easier overall because you get to move away from boring places and only show the most interesting parts from the most interesting POVs.

I have found multiple POVs actually decrease the difficulty level because every time you're stuck, you just cut away to another character, and days, weeks, or months could have passed between the last time you saw them.

The disadvantage is that you have to keep the main characters apart for most of the book. You don't want the MCs to see the same thing all the time. The book then becomes as much about how you keep characters apart as when you crash them together again to exchange the knowledge they've gained.

Of course, this again adds conflict because each main character gets to build their own party, but if you want your two POV characters together, you can't do that. They have to quickly be off on their own quests, again, like in *Game of Thrones*.

So, if you want to make a long series but you're completely overwhelmed by keeping the mythology straight, I recommend telling the story from many POVs to keep things interesting at all times, padding the word count, and then blowing up areas all the time once the mythology becomes too cumbersome.

SELF-WORTH

You have intrinsic self-worth just for being alive.

You are worthy of being alive simply by being alive. You don't have to make or do something to be worthy of that.

It has been the work of a lifetime to understand that my self-worth is not coupled to my success. It's not tied to my productivity.

It is not tied to anything.

It just is because you are.

OPINIONS

I understand and appreciate that everybody wants to help when you ask a question about writing or drawing, but not everybody's opinion is created equal, unfortunately.

If somebody is telling you, "write what's in your heart", but they have made negative money in publishing, or they haven't even written a book...their opinion should not be weighted as heavily as somebody who is killing it.

Similarly, if somebody hasn't made money in a decade, they should not be as heavily weighted as somebody making money now.

Caveat...if you don't care about having a career, doing it right, or making money, this advice goes out the window.

But I see every single day, multiple times most days, that people ask a question on a forum and then get 20 replies, 19 of them from people who "just want to help" or "give an opinion" but haven't even done one thing yet, and then ANOTHER person who has been through the wringer and come out the other side successful.

It's not a problem that everybody replies. It IS a problem if the dissenting voice is the only successful person, but you only weigh them as a single data point instead of the only data point that matters in that discussion.

You need to be savvy when you ask and provide opinions. Not all opinions are created equal. Not everything is a fact.

If a 20-year publisher tells you something, and somebody with ZERO or little experience tells you something different, they are not equal.

They just aren't.

That doesn't mean you should automatically follow what the publisher says either, but it should be given outmoded value compared to people who don't have as much experience. It's going to take A LOT to match the publisher's opinion because they are literally in the thick of it.

Now, in a different context, that publisher's opinion would mean nothing. For instance, if I wanted to know about Kindle Unlimited, I would not ask that publisher because they likely have little to no experience with Kindle Unlimited.

It's also important to weigh advice on how close their genre, release style, format, etc., match yours and weigh them similarly. Romance comics operate differently than action novels, and then both are quite different from children's books. Every genre and format has its own rules.

It is not the person giving the opinion's fault for giving it. It's yours for not understanding how to weigh opinions properly. This is not just true with other writers, either. It's also true with creating new work and asking for opinions from readers.

For instance, actual READERS of my work, and people who buy my books, are weighted SIGNIFICANTLY higher than somebody who doesn't when I ask a question about what to write next. You can use this with everything, but not every opinion is valid, and not all opinions are created equal.

"WHAT EMAILS SHOULD I WRITE?"

Q: I want a mailing list, but I have no idea what I should write in them. HALP!

A: One of the most important tools in your marketing toolkit is the mailing list, but it's hard to come up with something to write EVERY week. It's hard for me, too, but I write several TYPES of emails, and whenever I am bereft of ideas, I fall back on one of these topics. They are my secret weapons in the email game, so I use them often.

1. **Sales -** There are two types of sales emails. The first is the type that you write during your launch campaigns. Those should be scheduled out before your year starts, and if you block them right, then you should have a 2-4 week chunk of time where you know EXACTLY what you are going to write. The OTHER type is when you are running a sale on existing inventory, and while you should plan those out, it's never a bad idea to run a sale when you don't have any idea what else to do.

2. **Presale -** I spend a month before my big launches talking about the launch that's coming up, which means if I have a four-week launch, I have those emails PLUS the emails leading up to the campaign planned out. I run four launches a year, which means I have four months of sales emails and four months of presale emails already scheduled.

3. **Freebies** - This is a list of freebies I found on the internet. Since I'm an author, they are all books, but you can do recipes, art prints, or just about anything. These get HUGE engagement, but mostly from people who like free things.

4. **Five cool things** - These are five cool things I found on the internet. I spent the first two years of my mailing list doing this, and it's a GREAT way to start because you are always finding cool things around, and when you share them, people start to learn your taste, and you get a sense of what your audience likes to click on.

5. **My faves** - These are lists usually of my favorite books or comics of the year, or in the past month, etc. This is meant to get people to bond with your taste. Plus, hopefully, people on your list have ALSO had a positive experience with those things, and you can bond about your love of them. One of the best things you can be is a curator because if you can curate well and people like your taste, they will be more likely to buy your work when you launch.

6. **What am I doing now** - These are usually about my depression or anxiety, but they are the "real" ones that prove I am not a robot. Your email list is all about developing a deeper connection with you and your work, and it's sometimes important to talk about the things in your life that are important to you, like your pets, travel, or whatever you like to do outside of your work.

7. **Backstory** - Tell the backstory of a book, a project, or something like that. You can even tell stories of your past as long as it relates to your current project. This is meant to get people to have a deeper connection with your projects.

8. **Ray of hope -** This is when I take something from my life, tell a story about how it relates to their lives, and deliver a message of hope for people. A good email strategy runs on a continuum from "ALL about me and getting you to like me" on one end to "Here is my work, please go buy it" on the other. You need to play with it and end up somewhere in the middle, but sometimes you want to add something poignant and humanizing that will bond you and the reader.
9. **Lesson -** Like a ray of hope, but this one is some sort of lesson I learned I know will resonate with the people on my list—usually about how to get through a world that is cruel and unkind.

You'll also have your own spark of genius moments, but when you don't have anything and need a topic, these are great ways to prime your brain.

THE BELL CURVE

I have put off explaining this for a long time, but today is the time to explain the most boring and most important concept in selling anything.

You might think it's something like a sales funnel, which is monumentally important, but it is not nearly as important as the bell curve.

If you understand the bell curve, you can quickly understand all sales and marketing for any product.

I have a degree in demographic sociology, so I am intimately familiar with the bell curve, as I have worked with it since I was 18.

The general idea of a bell curve is that if given enough of the correct data on almost any subject, then the data distribution will look like a bell with a big, fat middle that tapers off on the edges.

Why is this important in sales?

Because ALMOST EVERYONE gives up on accumulating data before their distribution fits into a bell curve.

What do I mean by that?

Let us say that at a convention, every 100 people you talk to will lead to $100 in sales. Once you talk to 100 people, you can reliably predict you will make that amount of money almost every time.

The reason that is predictable is that you have found the normal distribution of your data.

However, if you give up and only talk to 50 people, you will not reliably make $50 in sales.

Why is that?

Because you have not spoken to enough people to normalize your curve.

You see, if you talk to 100 people, you might make that $100 from the first two people, or the last two people, or somewhere in the middle.

But by skewing your metrics, you no longer have a bell curve, which makes your curve more erratic and less reliable.

You MIGHT make $300 from talking to 10 people or $0 from talking to 70 people, but it's impossible to predict because you have not collected enough data.

The graph normalizes into a bell curve because there is enough data, a robust data set, to create such a curve.

This can't be overstated enough. IF you gather enough data, then your data will, 100% of the time, result in a curve that looks like a bell.

There are ways to correct for a less-than-normal distribution curve, but it's still partially a guess.

A bell curve is the foundational metric of statistics. It's how we can poll 1,000 people and make assertions about a whole population.

There is another factor working here, though, because to get a bell curve, you need your data collection to be RANDOM.

For instance, you can't pick and choose who you talk to at a convention because that is no longer random.

So, if you only look for people who look like your perfect customer, your standard distribution falls apart.

This doesn't mean you should go everywhere and talk to everyone, even at a supermarket or swap meet, unless they have a high propensity for being filled with your ideal clients.

For instance, if you want to study voting patterns in Texas, you wouldn't poll people in Oklahoma, right? So, you need to find the random distribution in whatever population you choose, like a specific convention.

However, it does mean when you decide to do a marketing/sales push, you need to get a ROBUST DATA SET. Otherwise, your numbers will vary wildly.

This concept is the foundational component of ALL sales. It's how you can predict the ROI of your ad spend, choose what conventions to go to, and how much money you will make next year.

People ask how I can so accurately predict my numbers, and it starts with having a robust data set.

When I go into a new situation, what scares me is that I don't have enough data, and I don't trust anyone else's data without replicating it personally.

So, how do you use this? Learn your numbers and talk to more people when you do a promotion.

Send MORE emails. Run MORE ads. Talk to MORE podcasts. DO MORE THINGS so that you can better predict your next launch and the next steps.

Your numbers might vary wildly from mine, but you'll be unstoppable once you know what it takes to get normal distribution for your launches.

I know this is a boring concept, but you can't have long-term success without it.

STRATEGIC PARTNERSHIPS

These last two weeks tried to kill me. You may have noticed if you follow my stuff that I have been just about EVERYWHERE. In these last 12 days, I have:

- Launched a Kickstarter.
- Launched a special offer for our Accelerator students (if you know, then you know).
- Launched a new cohort of our signature Kickstarter Accelerator.
- Relaunched my legendary viral builders with Booksweeps.

On top of that, I also had LASIK, and I have been recovering from that while launching 4x more projects than I normally launch. In fact, I'm pretty sure this would have been too much for me to handle even a year ago, and I would have collapsed under the pressure.

So, how did I do it and not curl up in a sniveling ball in the corner?

There was, of course, a lot of pre-planning, but there were also delays and other things that conspired to make all these things launch in very short order. I decided in June, for instance, to pull my Ichabod launch two weeks earlier to avoid the glut of huge books that normally launch at the beginning of September, which didn't help.

And, of course, there is simply the training to do the work. I know how to launch a Kickstarter, and I know how to build a webinar deck. I've done tons of webinars now, and I know how to write email sequences/sales pages. I can do all this work in my sleep (and some days in the past couple of weeks, it felt like I was).

All of that helped, but strong strategic partnerships made this possible. If you've followed me for a while, you might know that I have been besieged by terrible partnerships in my life until I didn't want to publish other books because partnerships burned me so badly.

Enter Monica, Ryan, and James. They are all rock stars.

James Emmett booked all my media for Ichabod. I've been reluctant to hire PR, but other people I hired this year to do my PR have been dynamite. I love doing press, but I hate booking press. It's held me back for a long time, so James has been a lifesaver.

Then Monica Leonelle is my business partner for WriterMBA, and Ryan Zee and I have partnered for these viral builders (though we have not made a new company to do so). There are many partnerships, and they all work a little differently.

So, how did somebody so averse to partnerships end up using so many of them successfully this week (and by all accounts, all the launches have been successful ones, including selling out of our builder launch in less than a day), end up in so many baller partnerships?

Well, I'll give you a couple of the best things that I've done.

1. RESEARCH

This was easily the most important thing, dwarfing everything else on this list. In my past, I got into a lot of partnerships hastily and got into more with people I knew were shady, but I thought it would be different with me. With all these new partnerships, I followed their careers for YEARS.

Aside from James, who I only knew through Twitter, I was friends with Monica and Ryan for years. I had used their services and products. Even with James, I knew the people he worked with, and they spoke glowingly about them. I did my due diligence not just by knowing them or using their products, but also knowing OTHER PEOPLE who had a different experience from me who used their services for a long time. They had a track record of stellar references and success.

Looking for partners who shared the same vision/occupied the same space as I wanted to/did occupy. With James, I knew he was an expert in comic PR.

With Monica, I knew we shared the same vision and had similar thoughts on how to get there.

With Ryan, he occupied the same space as me and wanted to add a new offering. In all three situations, I was looking for people who could complement my work and bring it to a new audience at the same time. My builders were well-received but only had an audience of about 200 people, while Ryan has helped 6,000+ authors grow their audience.

By working with him, I gained access to those people and allowed him to expand his business. With Monica, she was writing a series of business books that my work could fold into seamlessly and give her credibility in things like Kickstarter, while she could give me credibility with the entire publishing community that I had been unable to get during the first 10 years of my career.

I partnered with people who did the work consistently over time. I watched their launches and waited to see if they followed up over a long time horizon and kept their quality high. James was the person I knew least, but I watched him work with stellar indie books, and when it came time to hire somebody for Ichabod, I knew I wanted to try him out and see how it worked. These people DID THE WORK, so when I needed to offload a bunch of work to them, I knew they would follow through.

2. START SMALL

With Monica, it started with selling her my non-fiction work, something I had no intention of continuing without her. That might seem like a HUGE commitment, but compared to the business we started and the courses we've created, it's a small fraction of everything. Additionally, we ran ONE launch with her as my publisher and raised over $20,000. When we worked well together, it made sense to continue with something bigger; when that worked, we decided to build a company together. With Ryan, we started with a slate of 3-4 pilot tests to see if it worked, and we sold out in 12 hours. In both cases, we did a small launch, and it has worked seamlessly so far, so it made sense to continue with them into something bigger.

Our audiences were in alignment. Before working with somebody, at least on a big project, ensure their audience and your audience align. This is less important on anthology scripts or something small, but before you sign a big deal, ensure they have the audience you want and that your audience aligns with their goals. Do they publish in your genre? Can they help you get in front of a new audience? Is that an audience you want? Will signing with them amplify your work?

3. GET EXCITED

Whether it was their catalog, client list, platform, or something else, the things they were doing excited me and made me want to work with them. That's always the first thing I look for, that ember of excitement and drive to bring them into my orbit.

So, how can this work for you on a smaller scale? Well, ONLY work with publishers/creators who share your vision. This is how I hire sequential artists, cover designers, and just about everyone, no matter how big or small. I follow them for a long time, and when I see their hustle, we work together on something small, like the cover for one book, and then when that works, I expand into something bigger.

Either that or I work with people who were personally recommended by people who I trust implicitly and who I know have killer taste.

For instance, I generally won't sign with a publisher unless I know at least a half dozen quality creators who have worked with them and/or I have worked with them on a small project first. It's just the way I work. I have been burned enough that I have to be supremely cautious. I've signed many contracts in my life, and they are almost always for small anthology projects to test publishers or editors, and it's the same with them, I'm sure.

Don't feel the need to dive in with your whole body first. Try something small, go small, and know that your career is long. You don't want it marred with terrible people. You want to work with rock stars, even if it takes longer for things to develop.

Once your reputation is tarnished, it's hard to get it back, and that reputation is all you have in the end. It's why you have value to publishers and why your audience trusts you, no matter how small or large it might be right now.

CONVENTIONS AND BOOK SIGNINGS

Okay, people. I've gotten a lot of questions about conventions recently, so I'm doing a three-parter about conventions.

It's more apparent than ever that nobody teaches this stuff (except Monica Leonelle and me in our book *Get Your Book Selling at Conventions and Book Signings*).

So here is my down-and-dirty training on how to get your revenue/sales up.

First, there are some questions you MUST answer. You will never hit the next level if you don't know them.

- What was the total revenue of your show?
- What was the average spend at your table?
- How many TOTAL sales did you make?
- How much did you make per hour?
- What were your BEST hours?
- What were your WORST hours?
- What is the BEST day for your show?
- What is the WORST day for your show?
- How many people did you talk to to make a sale?
- How long are people at your table?
- How many pitches are you making to each person?

- Are you closing them on the first pitch or the second?
- How long before they walk away?
- Are you getting them on your mailing list before they walk away?

If you don't know these awswers off the top of your head, you can never get to the next level. You have to know your base number if you want to grow from it.

If it takes more than 10 people to make a sale, you need to hone your pitch and get better at finding the RIGHT person to buy your stuff. There is a profile for every single type of buyer, and it's not demographic; it's psychographic.

That means when you say certain words or phrases, the RIGHT CUSTOMER'S ears will perk up, and PSYCHOLOGICALLY they will engage with you.

You want to make at least 1 of 5 people buy. There is a saying that for every five people you talk to, one will buy no matter what, one will never buy no matter what you say, and the other three are persuadable if you say the right thing.

You really get great sales when you can get 2, 3, or 4 people to buy. That can quadruple your sales right there.

Then, you need to get up to $40/sale by doing better bundles. It's not reasonable to have a great sales day with only $5-$10 sales.

You generally can talk to 10-15 people/hr, and should average 3-5 min for people buying.

If you are having twelve 5-minute conversations on average an hour, that should lead to 2-3 sales, and you should be making $100-$120/hr on average.

If you aren't, you need to find a better-trafficked area, which will cost more.

You aren't going to make more than 3-5 sales an hour in AA or small press. There isn't the traffic to do it.

This is where pins and other low-cost/high-value things work to up the value of the cart. You can add them to orders to increase people's spending, OR you can add them for free when people spend a certain amount of money.

There are only so many things you can do to improve sales:

- Increase the average amount people spend at your table.
- Increase the volume of people walking past your booth.
- Increase the number of people who stop at your booth.
- Increase the percentage of people who buy at your booth.

This is an exhaustive list, though I think I missed one. I always think I missed one when I make these lists.

If you can double any one of those things, you can double your sales, but you can also stack them and 10x your sales given the right circumstances.

You can do all sorts of things to increase any number of those factors. I'm not here to give you the solutions. Monica and I give them in our book, but those are the issues and how you need to think if you're going to level up in 2023 and beyond.

I don't make the rules, but those are the rules. You can only do so much from behind your booth, and honestly, if you aren't going into a show with these ideas, you've already lost the game before the show even starts.

And finally, when you make these changes, you must be consistent. If you know you need to talk to an average of 10 buyers an hour to make an average of $100/hr, you have to do it EVERY hour because some hours you will make $300/hr, and some you will make $30/hr, but it will average out if you are CONSISTENT.

You need to know your numbers to build a repeatable system you can follow at every show and fall back on the numbers, whether the day is going well or poorly.

People ask me how I can keep going throughout the day, no matter what, and it's because I know that when things are going well, I have to ride it, and when things are going poorly, the only thing that will get me out of it is doing the work.

However, in fairness, it has been harder for me this year. I did SDCC on a cane, and it definitely affected my sales. It might not be possible for you to go this hard. I invented this method, and it's hard for me to do it, but you need to know some numbers, at least.

If you know and trust the numbers and work toward them, the money will follow.

My books are not considerably better than most others I see around me, but I'm willing to talk to everyone all day to hit my numbers, because I know if I do, then things will work out...

..and if they don't, then I will cut that show from my list and never return to it.

The numbers ALWAYS work when I'm at the right shows, and often even when I'm at the wrong ones.

GEARING UP

Since the show season is wrapping, I thought I would avail you of my convention strategy, going all the way back to when I started doing shows, as you plan for 2023 and beyond.

As you may know, I've had my issues with shows in the past year, but I still think if you are at the beginning of your career, you want to get to the next level as a creator quickly (aside from making better comics), and you have the spoons to do them, then conventions should be a big part of your plan.

I will always appreciate what shows did for my career, even if it is harder to do them now than when I started doing them.

Please note this strategy presupposes that you have a good comic but very few creators in your network and even fewer fans in your fandom.

Shows can quickly bring you an influx of awesome fans, but they have a physical and mental cost. So, please know that before you go into this process. It is physical labor to load books and speak with people all day.

A cost that may or may not be worth it depending on your life experiences. If you can do them, here is the strategy that built my career.

In all instances, if you are doing shows, you should ALWAYS try to speak on a panel/workshop. This will set you apart from just attendees/vendors and give you the stamp of approval from the show. This will help your relevancy.

This is all about how to be judged RELEVANT by the creator community. If you are already relevant or established, these rules don't apply to you, but if you've fallen out of relevance, then maybe they do.

Some of these are harder than others, so I ranked them, but if you want to be "relevant" to other creators, editors, publishers, etc., this is the game you have to play, especially at the beginning of your career.

1. GET A TABLE AT FCBD

It can be at ANY shop, but the whole industry looks at FCBD and judges relevance, so if you can get into a shop for FCBD, it looks positively on editors and other creators.

Difficulty level: 2/5 (this only comes around once a year, though, which is the problem)

2. GET A PRO BADGE AT SDCC OR NYCC

Generally, most other shows are regional, but if you can make it to either or both of these shows, then your relevancy score will increase. If you can get an AA or Small Press table, even better.

Difficulty level: 2/5 (pro badge), 4/5 (table/speaking on a panel)

3. TABLE AT REGIONAL CONVENTIONS

You don't have to go to every show in your area, but if you want to be judged relevant by your regional creator community, you should find your biggest regional show and find a way to get a table. Most people just buy a table, and you can absolutely find the vendor manager and just buy a table in most, but not all, cases. Depending on the show, it will cost you between $200-$700 for an artist alley/small press table.

This could be C2E2, ECCC, Planet, Megacon, Denver, DragonCon, NYCC, Baltimore, Rose City, Wondercon, etc., and your area might have multiple of them.

What you're looking for are the "hub convention(s)" everyone talks about all the time. Note, if you travel to shows, these are the ones you would do to gain relevancy in that market. It's not good enough to have "relevancy" on the national level. You also have to break into each region, as they have different rules and customs.

However, if you wanna know what shows I mean, it's the ones people always ask, "are you gonna be at X show?" when they talk to you.

Difficulty level: 1/5 (pro badge), between 1/5 & 4/5 (table/speaking) depending on the show, 5/5 (getting a guest table).

4. TABLE AT GOOD, LOCAL SHOWS AROUND YOU

These shows don't have big name recognition except in your city/area. However, they are solid local shows with a good reputation with creators.

Again, if you're trying to get into a new region, this would be the #2 thing to do. Start with the big shows, then funnel down from there into these types of shows. There will be a lower ROI, but this is where you meet and connect with real, hardcore fans.

These shows can also include themed shows like Gaslight Expo or Oddities and Curiosities Expo, which are much smaller than other bigger shows but perfectly tailored to your audience. I have a lot of success at horror conventions, for instance. I can make as much at a 5-10k horror convention as I do at a 50k comic convention.

These shows should be between $100-$500 for a table. The problem is that it's hard to know which ones work for you.

Difficulty level: 1/5 (attending), generally 2/5 (table/speaking)

5. DO SIGNINGS AT LOCAL SHOPS

When you have a new book coming out, call the local shops and do signings. Even if it's not coming out in Diamond, there will likely be at least ONE indie-friendly shop that would let you do a signing.

This should be free, but depending on the shop, they could ask for up to 60% of the sale of the book. Many shops will give you all the money or let you collect sales yourself.

Difficulty level: 2/5 (you have to call a lot of shops and get a lot of rejection)

6. SPEAK AT LOCAL WRITERS' CONFERENCES

This is further down the list, but if you want to boost your cred as an important creator, one of the best ways is speaking at a writers' conference in your area. Most areas have one at this point, and it's a great way to show that you have something to say.

I contact the coordinator of the show, usually not the showrunner but somebody on the volunteer or other relevant committee, and start a conversation. The more credits you have, the easier these conversations go, and if you're speaking at conventions, even local ones, it will boost your case.

You might offer to volunteer or attend the conference to learn before you speak at them. Usually, there is some good information there. I put this last not because it's not important but because it will ONLY affect your relevancy with creators, while everything else will also help your relevancy with fans.

This is ALWAYS my first goal at a conference, equal to selling books. My main goal is "How do I use this to boost my overall credibility in the industry".

Difficulty: 3/5 (you usually need some experience to do these)

You might be saying at this point, "wow, that's great, but you're talking about thousands, maybe tens of thousands of dollars. I don't have two pennies to rub together". Which is valid and why you need good books, a great portfolio, or some other way to break even or better at a show because it doesn't matter if it costs $10,000 to do a show if you make $20,000 doing it, right?

I mean, it definitely does matter because that's a lot of money to front, but if you can reliably make money at a show/book enough gigs to more than cover the costs, it makes the medicine go down easier.

BONUS: JOIN, OR START, A CREATOR ORGANIZATION

In Los Angeles, we have CAPS, which is national, but the local chapter is the main chapter. I was also part of a creator group that met at a local comic shop. If you have a local chapter or something like this, you should join it, as it will give you access to cool creators all trying to level up together. If you don't have one, then call on some shops and see if anyone would be willing to host you one night a week or a month.

Difficulty: 4/5 (building and maintaining a network is hard but rewarding)

Please note it will likely take a couple of years of running "the circuit" before you see any huge gains (the circuit being the group of shows you choose to do; many people will run "the circuit" of the biggest regional shows, for instance), but if you can do this for a couple of years, you WILL gain traction, especially if you spend this time to network with creators and build a fanbase by getting people who are interested onto your mailing list.

This looks different to everyone, too, but you can have a lot of impact in 5-6 events a year. Convention pros generally do 10-12, and I've done as many as 30-40 a year.

Over time this will evolve into a strategy you can use every year, but at the beginning, I recommend not doing any big shows you can't drive to, except for SDCC and/or NYCC.

If you want to learn more about what shows are coming up, you can rely on Conventionscene.com, or one of my favorite Facebook groups: Let's Do All The Conventions (And Take Over The World), or you can walk into your local shop and strike up a conversation.

Honestly, most shows are discussed by word of mouth between creators, so the easiest way to get into shows is to do what I said above and become part of the community.

If you want to learn more, you can get lots more in Monica Leonelle and my book, *Get Your Book Selling at Events and Book Signings*.

ABLEIST PROBLEM

For all the good conventions have done me, there is a pernicious problem with them as well. You see, there is a critical accessibility issue with conventions that I only realized at San Diego Comic-Con.

I can't, in good conscience, do a little series about convention selling without bringing this up because being successful at conventions is much more challenging for some people.

I have spent many days dealing with my chronic conditions and my wife's, but this was the first time I experienced a physical disability that forced me from giving 100%.

Or, I should say that my 100% was really maybe 50%.

Which meant I couldn't stand. I couldn't walk well. I used a cane and couldn't interact with new customers with my usual gusto...

...I realized during these interactions, where I was in pain, in grief, and not at my best, that unless you are standing behind your booth, smiling, and acting as if everything is perfect...

...90% of people will not buy from you, no matter what.

I always knew about the song and dance. I mainlined coffee to make sure I could stay up for it during the day...

...but experiencing it with a disability and age that prevented me from doing what I used to do was enlightening and disgusting.

This is not something shows can fix because it is inherent in the human condition.

People buy from the song and dance. They buy from the passion they can see on your face. If you are unable to provide that for them, they walk away.

Yes, I made sales, but they were mostly from existing customers who knew me and a few lovely humans who saw through the pain.

It's not fair, but it is the truth I saw that weekend.

I am astounded I never made the connection before, and I am very sorry for the ableist way I've been going about teaching convention sales for years.

The most important thing you can do for yourself is know your body and limits. It might not be profitable for you to do shows, which is okay. It's only one channel.

EVERY STEP

Every project you complete separates you one step further from your peers.

Even if they are bad projects, most people never make anything.

Even if they are just okay, that's okay. Most people never get to okay.

Even if they are good but not great, that's fine.

If they are great, even better, but every time you make something, every blog you write or page you draw separates you from all the people on the come up.

And then, weirdly, that body of work starts to speak for you. It overwhelms people.

They start taking you seriously simply because your body of work exists.

Meanwhile, every project finished is another one to put on the stack that people have to climb to get where you are.

Then, it becomes your job to lay the foundation for the next generation, to let them climb higher and faster than you.

THE BEST REVENGE

Trust me, the best revenge to a hater is finishing a book, making the next book, and then the next one, each time gaining more and more fans until you are so successful that there is no way your haters DON'T see your work everywhere and how many people love your stuff.

If you want to get revenge on somebody, then making increasingly more popular work until you have a stack of books so big you can't even cram it down their throat to choke them is better than retaliating against them.

In my experience, bullies LOVE being punched in the mouth; it gives them life and oxygen.

What doesn't give them oxygen is when people read your work and like it and then find out you are actually a good human.

There are plenty of caveats where this doesn't work, like abusive relationships and Twitter mobs, but for the overwhelming majority of human situations, when I find people engaging with trolls, I tell them to finish the next book and then the next one.

Haters want to fluster you, knock you off your game, and slow your progress.

Their narrative is that you are talentless and cruel, and the only way to show them otherwise is to be kind to everyone and create good work.

Stooping to their level is when they win. That is how they say, "See, they are a meanie."

They are filled with hate, and they are directing it to you. Their hatred is probably not even about you. It's from some deep-seated stuff. They need help, and you should block them, get away from them, and then keep moving forward.

In the same way haters want to hate, lovers want to love, and there are plenty of those, too. There are MORE of those, but they are quieter.

Haters lose when you keep going through it all and come out with a quality book on the other side. They lose when your support is so overwhelming that it drowns them out. They lose when your body of work can crush them.

I can't even fathom how many people have talked trash to me over the years, but they are all blocked, and I am focused on those people who support and don't drag me down.

I say don't engage from 10 years of being a lightning rod, responding to every negative person...until I just stopped and let the consistent work speak for itself.

CONTROL

Things you can control:

- Making your best work, every time.
- Putting together a team of people who you believe can fulfill your vision.
- Developing your unique voice.
- Baring your soul on the page.
- Continuing to create things you believe in.
- Doing consistent marketing.
- Finding new ways to engage with fans.
- Really connecting to fans.
- Reaching out to fans and friends regularly to check in.
- Connecting with new people in your industry that you find interesting.
- Keeping up with connections, both old and new.
- Maintaining a project budget and following it.
- Getting your projects done on time and within budget (usually).
- Being helpful and nice to everyone you meet until they prove unworthy of your help or niceness.

Things out of your control:

- How people will react to your work
- Whether your work will resonate

- If your work will blow up and become a huge hit

The only way you know for sure is to put it out and try your best. If you're lucky, very few things you make in your life will transcend the public zeitgeist and become hits that resonate with many people.

If I'm lucky, at the end of my life, the public will remember Ichabod, the Godsverse Chronicles, Writer MBA, and maybe one other thing. But, honestly, if something else comes on that's a bigger hit, something else will probably be replaced, and I'll no longer be known for that, at least to the general public.

My other work might resonate with certain people, but when people put together my obituary, those will be what people talk about unless something comes along and blows those away.

Most of my work languishes in obscurity. Some of what I consider my absolute best work never gets read.

Keep creating. Keep improving. Keep putting things out there, and keep trying to hit the bullseye every time, but you usually won't, which is why you have to be internally motivated and proud of your work regardless of the outcome.

Plus, if you are proud of it, you will fight harder for it, and you have to be a fighter to have anything break through and become a hit.

CREATORS AND TECH

There seems to be confusion about how tech companies have been screwing over content creators since the 90s. So, here's a quick play-by-play through our fraught relationship.

1. **A new hot tech company comes on the scene.** They immediately turn to creators and publishers, asking them to join their platform, saying they are "different" and are starting a "new paradigm" where content is king and creators rule. Amazon, YouTube, Facebook, and dozens of others did this at the beginning. They literally can't build without great content, so they are desperate. Amazon built its business selling books and now treats authors and publishers like garbage.

2. **Creators and publishers start to build out their platform, telling their fans to come to the platform.** The platform grows, and at the beginning, it's AWESOME. Money is flowing, and creators and publishers are happy. This is the last time publishers and creators will be happy.

3. **The platform hits scale, and suddenly the platforms don't need those creators or publishers because the platform is now bigger than any one or two creators.** Investors NOW want an ROI when they had been happy to funnel money into an incinerator before this point.

4. **Platforms throttle creators (Facebook), cut their revenue share (YouTube) or cut their rates for affiliates (Amazon).** Suddenly, those creators have a harder time reaching THEIR fans, the ones who, quite literally, built the platform in the first place. Yet, we've spent so much time building out THEIR platform we have none of our own.

Creators suffer so tech companies can get rich. They make billions while we go out of business.

Screw them. I will never, ever get tricked into helping a platform build its fanbase.

That's why I am so into my mailing list and Kickstarter, because at least there you keep your customer files, and they give you access to your own data. They are the ONLY tech company that hasn't messed with creators in my entire memory of tech since the 90s. That is why I am so rabidly loyal to them. They haven't even upped the percentage they take, like Etsy or Patreon.

Never trust a tech company that wants you to build its platform. They will screw you over 99.9% of the time.

It seems great at first. It seems too good to be true, and that's because it is.

TEN YEARS

Whenever somebody pitches me something, including me pitching things to myself, I find myself asking, "Am I willing to work on this for the next ten years?"

Because that's how long I've lived with most of my successful projects.

I used to say, "Let's try it" a lot, but as the pandemic has dragged on and I've had no choice but to look inside into the depths of my soul, I find that most of the things that have succeeded in my career had five years or more of build-up behind them, and I've been living with them for at least ten years.

I think you HAVE to say yes at first because you need to grow your skill, find your voice, and develop a body of work that you can be proud of, which takes a lot of effort. The weight of a decade would stop most young artists from even starting anything at all, but over time all those yeses have gradually turned to nos for me.

Ichabod started production in 2010, came out in 2014, and I pushed it until 2017 before it took off. The second volume releases in September 2020. TEN YEARS after I started it.

Katrina started production in 2011, came out in 2015, and took off in 2016. Then, *Pixie Dust* in 2017 and the

Godsverse Chronicles in 2020, almost TEN YEARS after I started it.

It's not just me, either. Almost everybody I know who's been successful has been working on at least one project for over a decade or more.

I used to start projects willy-nilly, not really thinking about the weight of what I was getting myself into, but the past year has taught me that every project has a life debt associated with it if you want it to be successful.

Even something like my anthology series started life in 2016, and I've lived with it for four years and three book releases.

It was immediately successful, which could happen, but it might be even WORSE if it's successful because then you can't abandon it, and you're forced to keep making things in that universe to keep paying your rent.

Those successful projects become what you're known for and what people expect of you.

I think about Arthur Conan Doyle a lot these days, a man who HATED Sherlock Holmes, tried to kill him off, raised his rates so high he assumed nobody would pay them, and became rich writing something he LOATHED.

There is now a statue of Sherlock Holmes across from Doyle's house, mocking him for eternity.

The idea of it haunts me every day. Yes, I am having many ideas during this quarantine, but nothing I'm willing to live with for the next decade.

Aside from small anthology projects, I don't think I'm going to be taking on much for a long time.

BOUNDARIES

About a month ago, I brought a proposal to a group I was part of. The idea was to do a virtual convention since we were all trying to build our notoriety in this space and I had experience running virtual conferences.

We spent about a month talking about it and planning it, and we were just at the first stage where people had to do homework.

I asked, and everybody agreed, to spend the next week writing 1-2 names per panel hour for who would make great guests to discuss each topic.

This wasn't a big ask, but it was the first step where I could judge if the people were good candidates for partnerships. It was something that could be accomplished in less than an hour.

This is where the boundary comes in. I set it without telling anybody because if people are notified of the boundary, it could make them more likely to complete the task to avoid punishment. It's essential to get a baseline assessment of the person to know if they are trustworthy or not.

If they all added names to the sheet, then they passed. If not, I was out. If somebody cannot do a simple task, then I can't trust them to do more or risk my reputation on them.

Note: it doesn't matter the reason why because there will ALWAYS be an excuse. There's also a caveat to this. If you reach out and communicate the problem, I am very understanding, but if you do not, then I assume the task will be completed as assigned and agreed upon.

So, what happened?

Only one of the three other people did the homework, and I've been part of enough partnerships that failed to know that's a red flag and that it's better to cut ties. Three companies blew up in my face because I chose the wrong partners. Not bad people, just not the right partners FOR ME.

So, I sent an email that said I was out because people didn't do the work.

Today, one of the people spent 15 minutes trying to convince me he wasn't in the wrong. He gave several excuses and even more reasons...

...but it didn't matter. That was a hard line, a boundary I couldn't cross.

It didn't mean we couldn't be friends, but it DID mean I was NOT going into business with him. I've watched that blow up in my face too many times.

Boundaries are important, and if somebody doesn't respect yours, you should find out early and get them out of your life.

This is how I go into everything. Small steps of trust with lots of ways to shut down, because otherwise you'll go too far down a road, and it NEVER ends well.

Ever.

He's not a bad person, just someone I shouldn't be in business with, and I am glad I found that out after 3 hours of work and not 300.

Do not let anybody push you around for having boundaries or make you feel bad about them. You shouldn't make them feel bad about breaking your boundary, either, but you should be firm and direct. Do not move your boundaries because if you do, people will think that your boundaries are flexible and will be less likely to take them seriously in the future.

I was excited about the project, but this is life, and the boundaries are more important to me because I know they protect me from worlds of grief. People have called me intimidating and hard to work with, but it almost always stems from the fact that I have clear boundaries and high expectations. I am reasonable if you communicate with me and if you can meet both my expectations and boundaries.

Mental health is more important than being liked, and I am liked by the people I care to work with, which is what matters.

SOARING HIGHER

The higher you get in a profession, the harder it is to get to the next rung. So, if the "success" in a profession can be tracked from 1%-100%, with 100% being the most absurdly successful person in your industry, then it's much easier to get from 80%-90% than it is to get from 90-91%, and every percentage increase gets harder still.

That's why it can take a year or less to get to 85% and then 10 years to get to 95%, and you might never get there because at the top are the biggest pros, the most successful people, and they are all incentivized to keep themselves in, and thus keep you out.

That's why publicity doesn't really work when you're at the bottom but DOES work when you're near the top because you already have some name recognition. Publicity gets you more exposure, as do press releases and other things that don't move the needle at all when you're just getting started. People toward the top, or at the top, are willing to spend lots of money to maintain their rank and get to a higher rank because they know that each rung on the ladder is smaller and more crowded than the previous one and can account for thousands, or even millions, more in earnings a year.

When you're playing with the big dogs, you need bigger guns because everybody is already using the smaller ones.

That's why the expression, "what got you here won't get you there" exists.

It's also when you have to ask yourself, "Am I willing to do what it takes to get there?"

The answer might be no, and that's okay, too.

I'll be honest. Earlier this year, I had to take a hard look at myself and say that I'm never going to become as successful a writer as I want to be.

Ever.

Because I refuse to play the game of publishing. I refuse to kiss a publisher's ring and wait for them to anoint me. I refuse to accept their terrible terms when they DO give me contracts, and I will not stay silent about their predatory practices.

Because of that, a publisher will likely NEVER hire me, at least not one with enough standing to push my work to the level that I aspire to, where I am a household name like Neil Gaiman, my work is studied in schools, and I'm seen as one of the greatest writers of a generation.

Honestly, I cannot and will not ever be that person, and it left me gutted for weeks. However, when I recovered, I realized that I could still be a successful writer with a devoted following of readers, who makes a good living, and that's more than other people could do with their lives.

I took solace in that because I understood what it would take to become Neil Gaiman, and I realized I wasn't willing to play the game to get there because it tasted bitter in my mouth every time I tried. Even if, in the end, I would be where I wanted to be, the journey there wasn't worth it to me.

I won't say I'm happy with the decision, but I'm at peace with it, and I've stopped fighting against it. I spent a lot of time wondering why I wasn't rising above my current station, and it was simply because I wasn't willing to do the things necessary to get to the next level, at least not by the current rules of the game.

Even in the world of self-publishing, there is a ceiling to how high I can soar because I write in an off-genre that has a natural cap on readers. I don't write to market, so while I can be successful, I will never be a seven-figure author because of the constraints I have put on myself. I had to become okay with that as well because I'm only willing to move to the market so much without compromising my work. The smart money is in writing to market and doing everything the hot trends are doing, but I can't write those books, which means I have to be okay with only being able to rise so high before I cap myself.

On top of that, because I have political and social views that I refuse to tamp down, I again lower the potential ceiling of my success. Again, this is something I have had to weigh and understand how it affects my career. Who knows how much that will affect things, but when you're talking about the top edge of success, even shaving 1-2% off is a considerable drop, and if it's 10-20%, that is devastating.

However, you have to make your own choices. Those were mine, and you will have to make your own based on your own values and interests, along with your own career goals.

You can't use the same tactics and expect to keep rising forever because there is a natural barrier where everybody is already using those tactics, and it's only NEW tactics that will allow you to rise higher. There are plenty of things I can do to become a more successful author, but I won't ever be the author I always wanted to be because I refuse to use the tactics necessary to do so, and that's okay.

It's okay if you make that decision, too.

SUCCESS

Success in any field comes down to a couple of things, and I will give them to you because I'm sick of watching the SAME questions pop up on every forum I'm in, on repeat, every week. Are you ready? Here's what it takes to succeed in ANY field, or ANY platform, for ANY business.

- Make something.
- Spend time building a community.
- Share your work with a ton of people in the right communities. Build friendships with people, not just surface-level platitudes. Help them grow and let them help you grow so you BOTH get to the next level and improve together.
- Make your work even better.
- Expand your reach into new communities and increase the impact in the communities you're already in. The deeper your connection with the people in your network is, the more they will want to go to bat for you. The goal, eventually, is to build your own community where YOU are the nexus point.
- Share your new work with a ton of people. If it's better, it will resonate MORE, and you'll be able to gain more aplomb for it. The more your work

resonates, the easier it will carry through communities.

REPEAT as many times as necessary, iterating along the way, making better work, building your network, and sharing your work until you break through to the next level.

This isn't a step system. Notice I didn't number anything. They are all things you need to be doing in tandem with each other all the time from the jump.

You can share your work by personally reaching out, joining groups, and forming collaborations, which is marketing...

...or you can do it through running ad campaigns, which is advertising, though I would probably hold off advertising until you have something that resonates with people deeply and have built a powerful network.

HOW you share your work might vary slightly between industries, but the underlying process is the same: network with people, grow your network, promote their work, have them promote your work, find more people, and repeat.

Podcasts, courses, comics, movies, television, novels, literally everything I've ever done works on the exact same underlying process. Conventions, Amazon, Kickstarter, your own website...ANYWHERE you want to grow your business, it's the same process.

If you aren't gaining traction, make better stuff, change the market for your work, network more, or share your work more, either through marketing or advertising. This is why series are a double-edged sword. On the one hand, a series that resonates can be magic, literally, a way to print money because every time you release a new entry is a chance to find a new audience and get the word out again. On the other hand, a series that doesn't resonate becomes torture as with every volume, people care less and less, and it can actually be a detriment to your career.

But seriously, what I wrote above is the blueprint. It's all you need to start making a plan. How you make something great, what communities you join, who you bring into your network, and how you iterate are very personal, but they should be the parts of ANY plan you make, and ANYTHING that doesn't fit in one of those categories can be cut immediately so that you can spend more time on the things that matter.

Unsuccessful people are CONSTANTLY bogged down with things that don't matter.

Now, you can stop asking in 1,000 forums. I have given you the secret of how to start ANY business. THOUSANDS of forum threads, HUNDREDS of conversations with successful creators, and my own experience have told me that in **every. single. scenario.** it comes back to those things. It's hard, which is why very few are successful.

THE "USEDABE" PROBLEM

There is a problem in authorship (both comics and prose) that I call the "usedabe" problem. It comes from people focusing on how things used to be instead of how things are right now.

You see, it used to be that if you made a decent book, properly packaged it, and placed it online, it would sell copies.

Then, the bar rose, and you had to write good books to sell them. Then it was great books.

Then, after the bar was raised on quality content, it turned to packaging. No longer could you just slap any cover onto a great book and expect sales. You needed a good cover, then a great cover, and now, you need packaging as good as anything coming out from trad publishers...

...and that's no guarantee of sales...that's just the bar of entry.

Even if you make a great book with great packaging, you now need to be great at marketing...

...and it still might not be enough.

However, the "usedabe problem" is pernicious because people are going over data, both collected and colloquial, that hasn't been relevant in YEARS.

Books are written in a specific place and time, but people buy and rely on them even if they were published back in the good ole days and haven't been relevant for years.

Even if the books are updated, they find the blog posts which support their comfortable lies, even if they were written five years ago. The only thing they care about is if the data supports their faulty opinion of how things should work.

Does it suck?

Yeah, it would be better if you could put an average book up and make money. I don't deny that would be much easier.

But that is not the world we live in, and you are setting yourself up for failure by not recognizing that and changing your plan to accommodate it.

Guess what?

It's the same on Amazon AND Kickstarter. It's been happening way longer on Amazon, but those same standards are still on Kickstarter, just on a smaller scale.

You still need a great book, well packaged, amazing marketing, and an audience hope to make a dent...

...and even that might not be enough. Even then, you can do all of that and lose.

It used to be that if you had all that, you wouldn't ever lose, but now, if you falter on any of that, you will almost certainly lose.

If you do it all perfectly, you still might lose, but if you suffer from usedabe, you are setting yourself up for almost guaranteed failure.

It leads people to make poor predictions of sales, to assume the algorithm will take niche books further than it has any reasonable ability to do in this climate, and to write books that aren't marketable enough to break even without extraordinary luck.

It used to be a lot different and will no doubt change a dozen times in the following years, but that does not make it better or worse...just different.

There are ways to exploit any system, but you must be able to properly analyze the system without "usedabe" clouding your eyes.

Otherwise, you will make costly mistakes that will take a long time to recover from, and time is the one thing we can't replenish.

POSITIONING

So, you want to "position yourself to take advantage of opportunities" instead of just "doing the work"? Then, there are some things you should know.

Positioning yourself is like a game of chess. To "check the king", you need to be making moves 20-30 moves ahead. Also, just like chess, you might do everything right and lose.

You only get 2-3 opportunities every year that can take you to the next level. The more levels it can jump you, the fewer of them you get.

Even if you successfully take advantage of these opportunities, you usually won't see the fruits of that labor for 1-3 years. I generally plan for every strategic partnership to pay off in 2 years, for example. They sometimes take less time (like my partnership with Monica) and often take longer or never pay off. It's best to assume you will gain very little, but plan as if you will get a whole lot. I was done with non-fiction when I sold my publishing rights to Monica, and it ended up better than I ever could have imagined. More often than not, it goes the other way.

Just because you sign a deal or "capture your king" (whatever that king is) doesn't mean it will pay off. Lots of deals fall apart, and many more fizzle, and you have to take that into your calculations, which is why you need to keep your own thing going even as you work on this bigger game of positioning.

The goal is to understand what opportunity you are trying to get a positional advantage on and the "board" you need to play on to win.

For instance, late last year, I finished a book called *White Rabbit*. It was a thriller, and I had never written a thriller before. I didn't know whether I did a good job, so I hired the most successful thriller author I knew to edit it.

I didn't know what would happen, but I figured if he liked it, it would put me in a position for good things, even if it was just knowing I wrote a good book that hit the tropes. Plus, I really wanted to work with this editor. Six months later, he started an agency and took me and the book on as a client.

Additionally, since every deal could blow up, it's important to protect yourself as much as possible. Always negotiate in good faith, but assume the deal will fizzle and set your contract up just in case it does.

So, always have a reversion clause, several actually, just in case things don't work out and you need to go on your own again.

Usually, you'll be working on 3-5 different "games of chess" simultaneously, unaware of which will work out but knowing that if you play enough games, you'll win enough times.

That said, if you take on too much, you will fail every time. Don't keep adding new things to your plate just because you can. If you constantly get distracted by shiny things, you will never have enough concentration to win any game.

Every time I pull back and do less, I find opportunities to do more with less.

It's important to note that if you play the game right, EVERYONE wins. You bring something the other person doesn't have, and they bring you something you don't have.

Most of the publishing deals I've signed this year or negotiated that fell apart were with companies that have distribution I don't have or a specialty that I can't exploit properly on my own.

Working with them brought me a person with experience in the genre I want to penetrate and an audience hungry for that kind of work. They get a well-made book that their audience will want and an author with a big audience to sell to for the rest of their catalog.

Though I likened it to a game of chess, it's not a game, or maybe it's more a cooperative game where you both get more out of it than you could alone.

The beginning years of doing creative work are mostly about making stellar books, building an audience, and becoming an authority in your space. It won't be signing 10-book deals with a publisher. No, it will be launching one book, getting booked at one conference, or even having a book signing.

Don't discount those, though. Running one successful Kickstarter campaign, for example, is a HUGE accomplishment, and the only way you can run 20+ is to run the first one.

What's even more interesting is that those set pieces where you win are also pieces on the bigger chessboard of your career. It all works in concert together, leveling you up and allowing you to stand on the back of your previous success to grow taller over time.

So, to position yourself, you might need to become a successful comic creator on Kickstarter, then at shows, and then have a successful podcast, or whatever.

Each of those is not only a big piece of positioning at the beginning of your career but ALSO a piece on the big board in the middle of your career. Everything is additive.

I spent years just growing my audience and becoming an authority to find the right strategic partnerships that would see the value of what I have to offer.

Now, I can play a much bigger game because my career was built upon those smaller wins.

Not to mention that now that I've mastered some of the other pieces of positioning, they become repeatable with much less effort. It took me YEARS to get into anthologies. I couldn't figure it out...until I did, and now I get asked most of the time instead of having to apply, and I can churn out good stories much quicker than when I started.

That's what I mean when I say these things build on each other. Now, that piece which is critical to audience building and authority clicked into place, and it still pays off even now.

The same thing applies to Kickstarter. I spent so long trying to figure out the anatomy of a $10,000 campaign, and now I regularly run $20,000 campaigns because once you lock these things into place, they become assets forever.

It's also important to note that understanding the board is as much about avoiding bad moves as it is about making good moves. It's about doing your research, knowing your numbers, and understanding what moves have a high likelihood of putting you at a positional disadvantage.

Working with a bad publisher, associating with creepy people, or getting involved in lopsided partnerships, usually borne out of eagerness, naivete, or desperation, can set your career back just as much as good moves can propel your forward.

The higher you rise in your career, the more positioning there is and the more patience you need.

.

"ENERGY FIRST" MENTALITY

Have you ever heard of a "profit first" mentality?

It's the idea that you take 10% off the top of your revenue for profit, and then you work with the remaining 90%.

I think in authorship, we need an "energy first" mentality, which means before we take on any project, we figure out how to retain 10% of our energy as "profit", so we always have some in the bank, investing and growing for us.

I am as bad at this as anyone (on both the profit and energy fronts). I was just about to go on sabbatical this year, and instead, I started a company with Monica that took all my energy.

I thought this year was going to be about restoration, and it instead became about transformation.

I'm not complaining about this year.

I have done so much, both physically and mentally, that changed me for the better and brought me to levels I've been struggling to get to for years. I've never eclipsed $150,000 in revenue before, and this year we more than doubled that, which is astounding to me.

That's in no small part, thanks to your support.

However, next year, I want to recover and make sure I always keep 10% of my energy just for me, so I'm building up a bank that will never run dry again.

Thinking, "will I be able to run an energy profit after taking it on" seems like a good enough place to start as any.

$1 TO $2

The success or failure of a business generally comes down to one statement:

Do I spend $1 to make $2, or do I spend $2 to make $1?

It can be as close as "do I spend $.98 to make $1, or do I spend $1 to make $.98?"

But people discount how important it is to drill into the numbers and know whether you are spending money to make money or making money to spend money.

I admit that I am very good at the business side of publishing, but my secret weapon is not building a mailing list or Kickstarter or courses or funnels.

My true gift is knowing how to be on the right side of that equation and not do anything that puts me on the other side, no matter how fun it might be to do it. It is in the ability to pour over spreadsheets and synthesize the data I find in them, which is a gift my father gave me.

I see the future through numbers, and it's why I'm still here.

Granted, it makes me a little bit boring. I don't do a lot of merch. I don't make big, flashy statements. I'm not doing $50,000 ad spends. Maybe it's hurt me as much as it's helped me in building our brand, but I'm still here; a very,

very, very small company in a brutal industry, after more than seven years, in a better position now than when we started, and that's something.

We've whittled our outstanding debt to less than $2,000 and have produced close to 50 titles, while I've personally worked on nearly 100 projects, if you include freelance and anthology work.

As we inch toward the end of 2022, I am spending a lot of time looking at numbers. Now that I have a brand new company, it's double the numbers making sure we are healthy for 2023. I'm validating the hypotheses we made last year and making new ones for 2023, but the bottom line drop dead number I'm looking at is whether we're spending $1 to make $2 or we're spending $2 to make $1.

I'd like to spend $1 to make $10, but that's not realistic in publishing.

This does not include Writer MBA, but I just pulled my profit/loss since 2016, and the top number is bigger than the bottom number.

Not much bigger, but bigger is a win.

During that time, I've employed myself full-time, contracted hundreds of artists, produced a metric ton of books (literally), traveled the world, saved for retirement, built a reputation, and right now at this moment, there is more money in my bank account than there was in 2016, or at any other time in our history.

Maybe it is my superpower. It is DEFINITELY the #1 thing that has saved Wannabe Press over the years, making sure my reach did not exceed my grasp.

THE QUIET MOMENTS

Do not believe anyone who tells you that you have to work all the time, hustle always, or do things you aren't comfortable with to get ahead.

The magic, I have found, usually happens in the quiet moments when your brain is resting, and rest is essential for clarity. Clarity, meanwhile, is essential for vision. And vision is essential for success.

More importantly, knowing where you are going is essential to not feeling completely lost. Having a guiding light lets you decide what to chase and what to let go of.

Sometimes, it's worth it to do something for free or even pay for something if it services your overall vision.

Sometimes, it isn't worth it to take a high-paying job that takes you away from your goal.

Yes, plans change, and visions always need to be adjusted, but without aiming for a point on the horizon, you will get lost.

And when you are lost and adrift, it's easy to get pulled in many different directions, to take on things that don't serve you, and not be able to jump on the right opportunities when they present themselves.

Life, I have found, is more about being silent and listening to the right opportunities and then being able to say yes to them when they come, much more than struggling against the current all the time, trying to be everything to everyone.

I won't lie and say you won't have to do that in the beginning. You have to swim, struggle, and build up your muscles. No matter how many times somebody tries to help you, it's almost impossible to avoid some pitfalls until you experience them.

However, you only have so many years on this Earth and so many chances you can take. I have talked to too many people who squandered their good opportunities because they were too busy mired in mediocre ones.

Yes, you do need to do a lot of work to get good and do a lot of things to get noticed, but the quiet moments, steeped in reflection and meditation, often yield the biggest results.

I take December off every single year, just allowing myself the freedom to play and do whatever it is my mind feels like doing. Usually, it comes up with some awesome stuff because I give it time to think and synthesize everything about the previous year.

Some people call it a luxury, but I think it's a necessity. It's hard in the moment to shut off my brain and watch my hard-earned money fly out without getting much back, but in the end, it's worth it because that time yields the absolute best ideas I've ever had in my life. The reason I have been able to scale so high so fast has not come from the constant shows and the other stuff.

Those ideas came from the 2-3 things I figured out in the quiet moments that allowed me to explode forward.

Some examples:

2015 - 1) I came up with the idea for Melissa the Wannabe, my mascot, which solidified my brand and our target customer for the rest of my career plus 2) my podcast, The Business of Art (which becameThe Complete Creative), came from that quiet time, which put me in contact with more high-level creatives than anything I've ever done plus 3) my show schedule and speaking schedule, which contributed to my break out year in 2017, plus 4) the beginning of the idea to launch the *Monsters and Other Scary Shit* anthology AND *Pixie Dust,* leading to easily over $100,000 in sales and were my break out hits two years later.

2016 - 1) I decided to run mailing list builders, which account for a HUGE percentage of my business (over $50,000 in 2019 alone), plus 2) I decided to write my first non-fiction book, which was the nascent idea behind The Complete Creative, and led directly to Writer MBA, plus 3) I decided to release *Monsters and Other Scary Shit* BEFORE *Pixie Dust* instead of the other way around, allowing me to build a huge list of people who loved monsters and comics plus 4) I had the idea of the *Monsters and Other Scary Shit* cover after struggling for months with an idea, and that became my #1 most commented on cover ever.

2017 - 1) I completely redesigned The Business of Art into The Complete Creative, along with launching Build a Rabid Fanbase, my signature course which has yielded over $20,000 in sales, and planned my other courses, plus 2) I decided to write 20 total books in 20 months, which taught me how to write really well, and I was able to launch a writing course earlier in 2019.

2018 - This was all about cutting things that didn't serve me. I cut a lot of small shows and marketing that wasn't working, and for the first time since I started, I was revenue positive for the first 11 months of the year and didn't need 1-2 big Kickstarters to save my year. I decided only to bring in that which made me stronger.

ALL of that came from taking December off, and those are the BEST decisions I have ever made for my company. They all came from stillness and reflection and allowed my mind to wander.

I still end up doing a lot of work in December every year, but it's work designed to let my mind wander, and it involves a lot of downtime to ruminate, think, and plan.

NONE of those are historically extroverted qualities. They are qualities most often associated with introverts. People often SEE the extroverted side of me, but the thing that HAS all the good ideas in the quiet, reflective, introverted side.

Every time.

Yes, that extroverted guy is the workhorse who gets things done, but the introverted one is the visionary.

A POWERFUL SHIFT

Next year, the most powerful shift you can make in your business is to stop thinking about YOU and start thinking about how everything you do should be received by other people.

How will this make somebody ELSE feel?

How will this project affect OTHER PEOPLE?

What is this meant to evoke in ANOTHER PERSON?

Why is this project important to THEM?

If you look at every meme that goes viral, it is ALWAYS about how people can see themselves in it or how they can see somebody they love in it.

The things that explode are not about the creator at all, in fact, but how the creator has molded something that makes OTHER PEOPLE feel.

Those things that REALLY connect are all about how the thing we made filled in a little part that was missing in a person's soul, made them feel whole for even a second, and made them feel like they were slightly less alone in the world.

Every project, during the creation, is personal, but the sooner you can start thinking about what sorts of feelings you want to evoke in OTHERS, the more successful that project will be, and the more deeply you can connect to others deep down, the more successful you will be.

Success is little more than many, many people believing strongly that YOU connect with a small piece of their soul that is desperate to be seen.

When they share something, they are saying, "LOOK AT ME! This matters to me, and if it matters to YOU, then we are part of the same tribe. If we can both enjoy this, maybe neither of us has to travel through the world alone."

Almost all creators can describe what their project is. Few can explain why it's important to them. A couple can discuss why they are uniquely qualified to make it.

Almost nobody can describe the feeling they are trying to evoke in their reader and why their work will make them feel a little less alone in the world.

Y ou would do well to think about how to switch your mindset so that you are worried less about what a project means to you and more about how it should resonate with the people who see it.

Personal resonance is absolutely critical and often overlaps with the resonance of others, but the more you can articulate your feelings and project them outward into the world, the more success you will have.

More and more things are made every single day, and soon AI will make even more than we could ever make on our own.

The ONLY thing we're going to have, in the end, is how our work makes others feel, how they look at what you do as a reflection of them, and how they feel less alone in the world when they think of the thing we made.

Even though every post I make is about something I struggle with or have struggled with, they are never about me. They are about taking what I wrote, and making them applicable to you, so they resonate with YOU and burrow deep down into your soul.

Sometimes, I am more effective than others, but that is always my goal, with every project, with every post, with every tweet, and with every move I make in the world.

If you resonate with what I do, it's because I've infused myself deep down into the core of every word I speak, but then my ego gets out of the way, and it becomes about how it can speak to YOU.

BUILDING A CAREER

A career is not built in a day.

It is not built in a month.

It is not even built in a year.

A career is built over a lifetime. So, why are you trying to force success this minute?

And why are you so upset that it is taking a while?

This stuff takes time.

WRONG CROWD

I was at a party recently, and I could not have been more uncomfortable. The party was loud, and I didn't know many people. It was the kind of place 21-year-old Russell would have gone to, but 36-year-old Russell felt out of place.

There was absolutely nothing wrong with the place I was at, either. The other people there seemed to be having a perfectly pleasant time. It was the right place for them, but I could not have been more awkward and ill at ease because it wasn't the right place for me.

I maybe said 100 words the whole night, which, if you know me, is not normal.

However, it made me realize that often there is nothing wrong with us when trying to connect with our audience. We are just in the wrong place, talking to the wrong people, surrounded by the wrong music, and dancing to the wrong beat.

In another setting, I'm perfectly pleasant.

In the right setting, you would have to pay me to shut up. In fact, just a few weeks ago, I was with many of the same people and had a perfectly lovely time chatting up a storm. However, when I'm in the wrong setting, I don't have the energy. It's the same for us in our creative lives.

Often, it's not that there's anything wrong with us. It's just that we're out of place. When we find the right place, we'll shine.

ONE HUMAN

There is a weird mechanic that occurs when most people start building an audience. As their audience grows, they start thinking of them as one collective, like a school of fish, instead of hundreds or thousands of different unique individuals.

This helps for academic discussions, but it's important to understand that every single person in your audience is an individual human with their own wants, needs, and desires.

I find it helpful to think of specific people in my audience when I'm writing. Often, I will write a line or develop a plot twist for one specific individual human, knowing they will get a kick out of it.

For me, doing this prevents me from thinking of my audience as a collective thing and reminds me that I'm writing for thousands of individual humans who share their love of my work in common.

It's daunting to write for a big audience, but writing for one human is pretty easy.

ABANDONED

Making stuff is hard. It takes so much time, effort, and energy that sometimes I can't believe we actually make things. Which is why it's so weird that once we make something, we move on to the next thing instead of trying to maximize the time spent on the things we've already made.

It doesn't make much sense. We spend days, weeks, months, or years making something, and then we spend a week or so launching it.

That's bonkers, honestly.

So, I'm making a pact with myself, right here and now, not to give up on anything I've spent time on, and I think is great. I'm not saying I'll focus all my attention on things I've already made, especially when they aren't money-makers, but I'm not going to leave stuff I've made out in the cold anymore. I'm going to keep finding ways to get new eyes on them and make a habit of revisiting old projects as often as I can to find ways for them to make me even more money.

Because I spent a long time making them, the least I can do is spend as much time trying to sell them effectively. I've tried to do this before to different levels of effectiveness, but I'm going to double down on this from now on and make sure all the time I spend making something I love isn't going to waste.

WHY ARE YOU DOING THIS?

I don't believe in the hustle-always mentality.

I think it is a recipe for burnout, and gleefully talking about working 20+ hours a day is not why I got into this game.

If I wanted to work 20+ hours a day, I would get a job. I work for myself so I can have freedom. Freedom to travel. Freedom to nap. Freedom to do whatever I want.

That is what I am working for, and it's important for me to remember that.

Your drive may be different, but it's important to know that drive so that you can come back to it.

It's easy to get lost in the weeds and just keep going, but I doubt oppressive work conditions are why you work for yourself.

Yes, sometimes you have to work when you don't want to or harder than you would like. Sometimes you will miss important moments, and sometimes you will hate yourself.

But you should always come back to remembering why you are doing this in the first place.

In that way, you will always be able to reset yourself to true north.

For me, it's freedom. What is it for you?

GET ON BASE

I've never been a home run hitter. I've never been one who had an amazing idea and knocked it out of the park. I've built my career on getting on base and letting good things happen.

I've hit a lot of singles in my life, and after I got on base, I've been able to make things happen. I've stolen second, then rounded third on an error, and since I kept moving along a little at a time, I have been able to score.

Every once in a while, I do knock one out of the park, but that's not normal. What's normal to me is trying to get on base any way I can so that I have a chance to score as often as possible. If I see a beautiful pitch coming down the middle of the plate, I will square up and knock it into the stands, but I'm never planning for that to happen. My plan is to give myself a chance to score somehow and put myself in a position to win.

In the end, it doesn't matter if you hit a home run or a single. What matters is how often you round the bases and score a run. Most people think there is only one way to run a business, but that's not true. There are plenty of people who look for opportunities and take advantage of them a little at a time.

Those little opportunities can add up to big things if you stack one on top of the other. However, few people talk about that because it's not sexy. Home run hitters are sexy. Getting on base isn't sexy, but they are both equally valid players. A team needs both, and you can make a hall-of-fame career getting on base and taking advantage of opportunities as they come up.

You don't have to swing for the fences. Often, getting on base is enough. Every time you get on base, you have a chance to score, and when you have a chance to score, good things happen.

.00001% BETTER

You don't have to like the person you were last week, last year, last decade, or even yesterday.

In fact, one of the keys to my growth has been my hatred for the person I used to be and working every day to become a person I can stand to look in the mirror every day.

I am often riddled with disgust for my former self. I hated myself until I was about 32 years old. Now, I moderately dislike myself, and I work every day to polish out the parts of myself I don't like and accentuate the parts that I do.

Nobody expects you to be a perfect human when you start your journey or even when you end it.

If you can be .01% better than yesterday, heck, even .000001% better than last week, the progress will be noticeable over time.

If you're anything like me, you will always hate the person you were, but you don't have to hate the person you will become.

OVERWHELMED

Sitting here in my poorly insulated house, curled up as tightly as possible, waiting for the fireplace to heat my room to a respectable level, I have been reflecting on this past month and all the people we've met along the way. Whether at RAM in Houston, 20Books in Vegas, or online, there has been a constant fear that weaved its way through every conversation.

No matter their stage of success, people nearly unanimously said "I am overwhelmed".

By the sheer scope of what there is to learn about publishing, the constant pressures of life beating down on them, the shiny ball syndrome, or the desire to get to the next level but having no idea how to do it.

No matter how the overwhelm came, it was there in almost everyone.

Many of you have tried every platform without success and have very little energy left to try something new. Some of you are just beginning your journey into publishing, while others have been doing it for years. Maybe you have an outline of your first book, or maybe you've written 100.

In the past month, I've watched seven-figure authors break down in tears from overwhelm and seen six-figure authors on the verge of a panic attack at the thought of adding something else to their plate.

I was talking with a successful author coach at 20Books, and she said something instructive. I might get the numbers wrong because every day of this month feels like a year, but she said that in most industries, the burnout rate is something like 10%, while in publishing, it's more like 50% (and I think it's more like 70%).

Monica and I often talk about how, given enough time, every indie author will burn out. Writing a book a month, commoditizing your books to feel like everything else instead of the unique piece of art it is, constantly feeling behind the eight ball...

...all of that commingles together, building and building until the weight is unbearable for nearly everyone.

I personally feel like I was sold a bill of goods about being a writer by every movie and TV show I've ever seen; that of an author sipping tea at a lake house, writing one book a year, and getting to do whatever they want, without a care in the world.

They never talked about the oppressive writing deadlines, constant marketing, or even the schlepping books to the post office every week. I never ever thought more than half my job would be logistics when I first started, and I definitely didn't think I would be expected to write a book a month to stay afloat.

I won't lie...that pace burned me out. I haven't written a book since June, and before then, I wrote almost a book a month for two years. It's an impossible pace, and I don't wish it on anyone.

Truth be told, being in constant launch mode on these courses since March took me to the edge of burnout this month...and I didn't know you could burn out while you were burned out.

The good news is that both Monica and I know the warning signs of burnout, and we've been able to monitor the situation and make plans to pull back from the edge in the future.

And honestly, if I could break down WHY you should work with us more than anything else, it's because we've been through just about every possible part of this industry. We know how to navigate the mental, physical, and emotional aspects of living a creative life.

The reason I love Kickstarter is because it allows me to make more money from fans who love my work without forcing me to work 100 hours a week.

Functionally, it doesn't matter if it's Patreon, Kickstarter, or Schlamborken (a fictional site that doesn't exist). I'm mostly interested in protecting my energy and spending it on the people who love my work the most. I'm mostly interested in creating an author ecosystem which works for MORE authors.

I want to see my wife, play with my dogs, and love my life without being stuck to a computer all day, every day, pounding out 5,000 words a day until the magic of the art form I love is beaten out of me.

Yes, currently, Kickstarter is the center of that...but that's because Monica and I have seen everything in publishing over the past decade and have never seen a platform so primed for authors to take control of their careers and mental health.

Yes, we do show you how to make money on Kickstarter, but what we are REALLY trying to do is teach you a way of existing in the publishing world that prevents burnout, gives you the power to control the trajectory of your career, and make the money you want without publishing a book a month (unless that's how you want to live, then, by all means, do you, boo).

Kickstarter gave me a career, yes, but I have launched books every which way but loose, and when I tried to launch the traditional way, my mental health got so bad I nearly had a breakdown. I probably wouldn't be here today if that were the only way of making a living as a writer.

The ONLY thing that stopped my breakdown back in 2019 was going back to Kickstarter, where my biggest fans showed me my work really did have value. It literally saved my life.

It's not the only way, though, and I recognize that. Both of us recognize that.

Russell Nohelty

THE DRAGON

There is an old parable about a dragon and a door I think about often.

Walking through the door is easy. It is as simple as turning the knob and putting one foot in front of the other.

However, that door sits at the tip of a mountain, guarded by unknowable terrors, booby traps, and magic.

It will take all your cunning to navigate the path. You will need armor and weapons. Even then, the odds you will survive are minuscule.

You will face obstacles that work to break you and ones that will surely destroy the person you are today…

…but if you defeat the dragon at the top of the mountain, they will drop a key, and then walking through the door is easy.

I think about this every time I have success doing something because every single time, it felt impossible. I had to remold myself into a different human than I was and fight like the dickens to gain an inch.

I faced things I thought would break me, and frankly, they did. They wretched me apart more times than I can count, and I had to reforge myself with every rending of my soul into something new.

Some of those things I abandoned. They weren't worth the fight. I accepted, for instance, that I will likely never direct any more movies. That mountain was not worth the sacrifice to me, but it might be for you.

Others, like writing books and making comics, I worked and worked and worked at for years. I fought every battle, and it molded me into something different than I was before, a better version of myself, one that could easily summit that mountain.

Eventually, I did reach the summit and walked through the door a success. Every time I thought to myself, "Wow, that was easy. What was I so worried about all this time?"

But it wasn't easy. It's just that I defeated every obstacle to get there.

Of course, when I walked through that door, all I found was another mountain to climb, but that's a parable for another day.

BUY-IN

One of my key goals is to get somebody to follow me on as many platforms as possible. Every time they opt-in to hear from me, they are buying into my brand. Buy-in does not necessarily mean buying a product. It means they have built trust in your brand and are much more likely to buy from you in the future. Buy-in now means buying from you later.

Thus, my goal is to get as many buy-ins from a potential customer as possible, as often as possible.

If I can get somebody to download an ebook, for instance, they are much more likely to buy than just joining my list and doing nothing except receiving my emails. If I can get them to join a giveaway or follow me on Facebook, I know they are even more likely to buy from me because they are engaged.

The more times they choose to engage with my brand, the better a customer they are in the end.

This is not always true. Sometimes a customer never engages and still buys every time I offer something. However, that happens far less often than with somebody who chooses to engage with me more often.

I'm not judging them based on the immediacy of how they buy. I care much more about how committed they are to buying every time I release a product. Every time they opt-in to hear from me, it's a little commitment that they like and trust my brand, and people who trust me are exponentially more likely to buy from me.

Will they buy everything? No, because some things won't fit their needs. I write fantasy and science fiction books and comics, along with selling courses and marketing services. Some people do want all of those things, but most people are only interested in a segment of my offerings, and the more engaged they are, the more likely they are to buy anything that comes along which suits them.

If you're looking for your best buyers, they will likely be the ones who follow you everywhere and join every promotion you offer. When you have that kind of buy-in from customers, it's just a matter of scaling it.

QUIT

If something doesn't serve you anymore...

...quit.

Sick of writing? Stop writing.

Burned out on painting? Give it up.

Lost your joy with entrepreneurship? Get a job.

Stop. Burning. Out. To. Prove. Something. To. Yourself. Or. Anybody.

There is zero shame in quitting before you drive yourself into the ground.

If you regret it, guess what? You can start doing it again.

Have more time? Pick it back up.

Realize it DID serve you? Get back on the horse.

But never, ever feel bad about letting go of something that doesn't serve you, no matter how much time you've put into it. Life is hard enough without being shackled to something you don't love.

NETWORK VS. FANS

You need a network of fellow weirdos to go through this crazy existential existence with, grow with, learn with, and level up with, so you can reach success together.

You need fans who love your work, buy your work, and happily talk you up to their friends.

A network is a finite resource. You can't have millions of people in your immediate network because you have to nurture and care for it.

A good network has limits.

You can keep maybe 200 people in your close network at any one time because you need to reach out and engage with them.

A fandom is infinitely scalable because you do not have one on one interactions with them on a consistent basis. When you do interact with them, it's often to address them as a group.

Hopefully, your networks are fans of your work and vice versa, but they are two distinct things, and you will screw yourself if you treat them like they are equated.

BINARY GAME

Life is not a binary game. You don't either win or lose, which is a troubling thought when you are on a hot streak and a comforting one when you are on a losing streak.

Your biggest win can be followed by your greatest failure, and vice versa, but usually you will go months, or years, between peaks and valleys, where you will neither win nor lose but exist in a nebulous state of worry, wondering when the other shoe will drop.

You will give all your effort to some things and fail, and then you will barely try at all and succeed at others.

The more effort you put in, the more chances you have to succeed, but like the lottery, buying tickets just increases the odds. It doesn't guarantee success.

The more things you try, the more chances you have of cobbling together an interesting skill set that will make you the best in the world at something. Even if that thing is not particularly useful, it will be useful to somebody, and if you are the best in the world at it, somebody will likely pay you for it.

My "stack" of skills is very, very weird; crowdfunding + conventions + giveaways + book marketing + writing + comics + anthologies + editing + lecturing + courses + social media + email marketing + podcast.

I am the best in the world at that stack of very weird skills, yet I have been able to make a six-figure career from it specifically because it is so niched down that nobody else cares to do it except for me, which means when somebody seeks that combination of skills, I am the only name on their list.

TRASH

The easiest way to make new fans is to send them something that exceeds their expectations.

The easiest way to lose fans is to send them something that's disappointing.

The difference in cost between the two is usually not that much, but the difference in emotional resonance is HUGE.

Step one (before any of the marketing stuff I talk about) is to make something so good they can't ignore you; so good that, when somebody sees it, they go, "Holy crap. What is this?"

Then, you have an unfair advantage over everybody else.

Without that element, though, all the marketing in the world will only do so much to push your trash, or even mediocre, product.

The minute you start making things that are head and shoulders above the average, things that are easily best in class, then the rest of it becomes easy.

The rest is just showing people that your work is CLEARLY better than anything else out there.

I do think people wait too long to start marketing their stuff, usually way too long.

However, it's depressing how often I receive a Kickstarter and am let down by the packaging, the lettering, or the little things that are EASY to fix.

Packaging is SO EASY.

It's pretty cheap in the grand scheme to go from a 50 lb paper to an 80 lb paper (when working with the right printer), to get a better cover, or hire a better artist, to go from the cheapest printer to the best one, and, if you're ready to go offset, to go from softcover to hardcover even.

Yes, it is more expensive, sometimes quite a bit more expensive, but the ROI on those upgrades means everything in the court of public opinion.

You don't have to hire Neal Adams to draw your book, but I see the trash art in most of the books I get, and I sigh. I see the piss poor editorial decisions and shrug. I see a cover that is so clearly gross that it's hard not to gag too much. Every show is littered with bad packaging.

Or even mediocre art and story. Stuff that's not good, but it's not bad, either. It's just...forgettable. Honestly, most stuff these days isn't bad. It's just forgettable, and that used to be enough. If you could be serviceable, you could make a career, but now, you have to be the absolute best if you want to get noticed.

I see it all the time on Amazon and Kickstarter. Books that are...fine...there is nothing wrong with them. They are technically quality art, but there is nothing about them that makes them stand out.

If you want that next-level money, you HAVE to stand out. You HAVE to be the one people talk about. You HAVE to make your books so good that people have to share them.

Most things are forgettable, and if you are forgotten, you will fade away, and NOBODY will talk about you.

Those books go in my "well, I'm not buying one of those again pile" or into my "support because they're friends but never read pile".

An exceptionally few books go into the, "I have to buy everything they ever do" pile, and if you can't get into that pile, you just AREN'T going to get traction for the long haul.

That should be your only goal.

Not a week goes by that I don't hear, "Did you back x campaign? I just got the package, and it looks like garbage."

And then I know never to back that person again because first impressions matter. Even worse are books that elicit NO REACTION AT ALL. They are nothing burgers. Not good. Not bad. Just forgettable.

I think about this with everything I do. When I speak, my job is to be unforgettable so that people remember my name. I can't just be adequate or passable. I have to be so good they can't ignore me. When people ask their favorite speaker at a show, it needs to be ME because that's how I get invited back.

Otherwise, I'm lost in the noise.

If you can make somebody go, "Wow," before they've even opened the book, your work is like 50% done for making a fan.

But it's clear that most people, when given the chance to impress, just don't care.

And it's the dumbest thing ever. I just got a package from my friend filled with the books I got at NYCC last year, and I can't tell you how disappointed I was with the packaging of all but a select handful.

I have no interest in reading most of them, which means when I DO read them, I will have a bad mindset going in, and they will get less of a chance to capture my attention.

This business is SO hard. You have to give yourself EVERY opportunity to succeed.

Usually, less than $500 here or there can turn a book from average to great, which sounds like a lot on the front end, but for something you will have FOREVER and be able to sell FOREVER, it's not that much. It's a nip there and a tuck here.

Those little investments help you make a book SO GOOD that people can't stop saying, "Wow! What is this, and how do I get more of this tomorrow, please?"

When people want more, they will buy the next book, and if that one is good, they will buy the next one, and so on.

It's insulting to get something ratchet, and the last thing you want to do is insult people, especially when it's so easy and impressing them is so hard.

Therefore, when you DO impress them, you'll reach an elite class that only a few people go into, and the rest becomes SO MUCH EASIER.

This is the artisanal craftsman part of the publishing business. It's why historically, artists and writers are considered craftsmen, like blacksmiths or cobblers. Artisan is right there in the name ARTIST.

Russell Nohelty

An artist is an artisanal craftsman.

That's why we call it the craft of writing and why the whole process matters from end to end, not just the construction of the book but the packaging as well.

The finished book is the object we sell—the WHOLE BOOK.

Books are an object, a totem, that gives you a chance to delight people, and you will be messing up big time if you send trash books to people.

Or worse, you send forgettable books to people that don't even elicit a reaction.

Nine times out of ten, when somebody asks me why books don't sell, I have to bite my tongue to avoid asking, "well, is your book trash?"

Because if it looks like trash, then there's nothing I can do. If it's awesome, then there's everything I can do.

RETHINKING SOCIAL MEDIA ENGAGEMENT

The dichotomy of social media engagement is that a plurality of posts that get good engagement are terrible for converting sales, and posts that are great at converting are terrible for engagement.

This is not true every time, but 60-70% of the time, this will bear out.

It happens less when you are showcasing art, more when you are running Kickstarters or other launches, and way more if you are just posting a link instead of an image.

You might say, "Well, that means 30-40% of the time it works, so I should keep doing it", but when you run a company at scale, it means you'll be losing more often than you win, and that's not a good way to run a business.

Engagement is great for the social media network, but it's useless for running a business, at least during a launch, when most product-based businesses care about making money.

Yes, it's nice to engage with people, post stupid memes, and get reacts, but social media engagement is a hollow metric at the end of the day because it, by the factor of the above statement, is a horrible way to judge sales.

There is value in engagement because it builds empathy, trust, and likeability with your audience. I love Facebook for audience engagement, but I do not expect it to be a sales driver unless I pay for ads.

I love engaging with my audience, and I'm thrilled to do it, but if you judge your posts by REACTIONS, especially SALES POSTS, you're going to be sorely disappointed by the results.

Posts that CONVERT get AWFUL engagement. People that click, rarely also engage because they have ALREADY clicked off the site.

They are going to buy, so there is no need for them to click the react button.

People perform one action. So, if they are engaging, they are not clicking, and vice versa. The reason sales posts get good reactions is that people run them into the ground with ads, and by the sheer volume of exposure, they get a lot of reactions, not because they are great at organic engagement.

When you are running ads, you can even tell Facebook you are looking for engagement, clicks, or conversions, and it will target different people depending on what you choose because engagers are, generally, NOT buyers.

Ironically, this plays into the algorithm perfectly because it judges success on reactions.

Reactions mean people stay on the social network, and staying on-site is essential for a social media company's market capitalization.

They want to make it very difficult to get off the platform unless you pay for it.

Thus, posts that CONVERT do not matter to the algorithm because they do not get reactions and are thus naturally suppressed, forcing you to buy advertising to promote it.

Thus increasing a company's revenue and valuation. Unfortunately, most people equate reactions to sales and factor the wrong things into their plan, meaning their campaigns are doomed before they begin.

HOW TO TELL IF YOUR WORK IS ANY GOOD

The problem with being a creative human is that the act of doing a thing makes you better at that thing, so we will naturally think our work isn't good enough forever because we always get better in the making of it.

That being said, I consider "being good" the ability to move people with your art. So, if you are moving people, that is a good sign.

Practically, buying intention is a good way to judge whether your work is good. Buying intention is different from praise. People offer praise very quickly by saying things like, "Good job" or "I liked that".

Buying intention is different. Buying intention is almost a visceral reaction. When people say things like, "I never PM people to talk about their work, but I loved this!" or "When is the next one coming out?" or "How can I buy this right now?"

Once, I was showing David Gerrold one of my books. I wasn't trying to sell him. I just wanted to show him that I was an author, too. During the pitch, he opened it and started reading the first page. After reading it, he said, "Yeah, okay, this is good," and handed me $20 for it.

To judge good, I look for whether my work can sway people to action, not just shallow praise. Another great way to tell if your work is any good is if people tell others about it. Word of mouth is a great referral source, and people tend not to refer garbage to each other. Often at shows, my fans will drag their friends over and nearly force them to buy my work, which is one of the nicest compliments I can receive.

I try not to judge a book by its sales because my favorite and most beloved books by readers are often my lowest sellers because they are not traditionally marketable. I can judge by buying intention, though, and the visceral reaction somebody has when they read my work.

VILLAINY

Sometimes your job is to be the villain of somebody else's story.

It sucks.

I'm not saying you should become a mustache-twirling ne'er-do-well, but as you go around the universe and exist, you're accidentally (I hope) going to do something untoward to somebody else.

Likely, you won't even know it.

Probably, in your own eyes, it won't be bad, but it will be, and even if you realize it later, there's roughly zero you can do to make it up.

In the best situations, you will be a motivating factor in somebody else's growth, even though you will never be a hero to them.

That person you fired, even if it was to save ten jobs, won't EVER think you are a good person, no matter what you do.

Or that editor you didn't hire because you went another way is never going to look at you in a good light, even if they understand.

Or even when your book launches better than somebody else's, they will look to YOU as the bad guy, even if you earned it.

Or maybe you accidentally cut somebody off, hung up on them, unfriended them on Facebook (or didn't confirm their request), or just passed them over, not looking their way.

Any number of innocuous things that happen during the course of a day that we barely think about could make you the villain in somebody else's story.

While we're forging the heroic path for ourselves, we're becoming the villains in other stories all over the place. I cannot overstate how much this sucks, but it is part of growing a business.

You should always try to mitigate any negative you put into the world and try your best to make up for what you've done.

But sometimes, somebody won't forgive you.

Sometimes, they shouldn't forgive you.

Sometimes, you will be the bad guy.

And that is your role in that story.

It doesn't mean you're a bad person just because you're a bad guy.

Don't get it twisted, though, sometimes you are just a bad guy, and in those situations, you need to look yourself in the mirror and have a reckoning with yourself.

This is not carte blanche to be a dick. Quite the opposite, in fact, but even if you do everything right, you're absolutely going to come off as a villain sometimes.

You should always try to do the right thing anyway, but occasional villainy is a side effect of existing in the world and trying to succeed. You created villains out of people, and so too, will people make villains out of you.

And you just have to sit with that and exist knowing it, trying not to let the thought fester inside of you.

MARKETING THAT WORKS WELL

The problem with marketing is that most of the bad advice works short term and not long term, and most of the stuff that works only works long term and not short term.

People who hate marketing generally fall into two camps.

1. **People who have decided to "dip their toe" into something like ads or mailing lists, but not for long enough for them to actually work**. Then, they complain that those things don't work, even though they only did them for like 3 months, or only send an email once a year, and don't even optimize it when they do.

2. **People who tried some garbage, saw it work for a minute, watched it flame out, and are now so bitter they think nothing works or that something that works won't work long term.** If they are still doing marketing, it's at such a small level that they could never survive. Maybe they rely on newsletter swaps, which only work when stacked with a bunch of other promotions, or they post on social media, which only works...well, pretty much never unless you have a stacked profile, but usually they do nothing.They sure like to tell you what doesn't work, though, and what could never work just because it doesn't work for them.

I've written two books on this subject and pretty much dedicated all my free time for five years to the study of building a creative career. Successful people do the things that work for long enough for them to work, and while they might try out new strategies, they are aware, for the most part, they will flame out.

Most every successful creative I know has a mailing list (even if it's a small organic one of a blog that hosts subscribers they can reach during a release). They have 1-3 social media accounts which have a robust follower base, and run ads at least at some point during the year.

How they function otherwise is different between them. Some have podcasts, Youtube, or a blog. Some focus on releasing products ALL THE TIME, like all the time, so much of the time that it feels like they couldn't ever sleep.

Those people take the energy I use for podcasts and doing other things and focus it all on making and launching their products, and that becomes their consistent content.

Some do big launches, and others keep it small.

But what is consistent across ALL of them is:

- Mailing list (or blog with a subscriber list they can reach during a launch).
- 1-3 robust social media accounts.
- Advertising (this might be on Facebook, Google, in the newspapers, on the radio, or even at conventions).
- Launching GREAT (not mediocre or good) products consistently that their audience WANTS.

Most of them have either a YouTube channel, a blog, or a podcast, but not all of them. In fact, not nearly enough of them for me to say it's required unless you want it.

All of them do the four things listed above and constantly talk about how they wish they had done them all sooner.

You can complain about it, argue, or say it's not worthwhile to do one of those things, but I have spent my professional life looking for trends in marketplaces, and those four things are consistent EVERYWHERE I look. Are there exceptions? Yes, but the massively successful ones all look pretty much the same, though not exactly the same.

Literally, everywhere, so when you say one of those things doesn't work, I know what you mean is, "this doesn't work for me, and instead of looking inward at myself, I am blaming the mechanism".

I have seen people succeed without doing one of the things on that list, but the most successful ones do all four. Besides, even if you could "get away" with just three, why would you not want to give yourself the BEST chance of success?

TREATING HUMANS LIKE HUMANS

It's a radical idea, but people enjoy being treated like humans and not walking wallets.

In fact, customers buy from people they like...and they tend to like people who care about them.

And I am sure you want to treat your fans like humans...but do you? Do you really?

I don't know the answer to that, but a surefire way to stand out against a field of other creators is to show your love to the people who will support you.

There are all sorts of ways to do this, from offering freebies to giveaways to hosting live streams to conversing with them in a Facebook group.

Even just asking questions and listening to their answers is something more than most people do right now.

You don't have to bend over backward and spend every minute proving you care, but you should do something, sometimes.

In a world full of companies treating their customers like walking wads of money, treating your customers like humans is innovative.

ROLLER COASTER

I've been thinking about my career a lot as I near my 40th birthday. For the first time since I started doing this, I finally feel like I'm in a good place. It might not last, but it finally feels possible that this could be a long-term career for me.

It's been a wild roller coaster of a ride that often felt like it was going to pop off from the tracks, and other times seemed that there were no tracks at all.

I know many of you are struggling through that "trough of obscurity", wondering if there will ever be a light on the other side, so I thought I would show you all the ups and downs of my own career as best as I can remember them.

Here is a short rundown of the biggest "hits and misses" of my career up until this point, starting all the way back when I was 18, through today. I tried my best to get the dates right, but I may have misremembered some of them.

As you will see, there were a LOT of misses at the beginning, and the bad dominated the majority of my career until recently.

2001

06/2001 – I graduated high school. I wanted to go to NYU to film school, but couldn't afford it, so I settled for journalism school at the University of Maryland, where I made a very mediocre to straight bad documentary called *Culture Shock*. I won an award for best director for that one, and I think my teacher regretted giving that to me when it was all over.

2004

12/2004 – I graduated college, determined to make films, even though I had never made a film. I did a lot of journalism in school, though, which I think helped me a lot in what I do now.

2005

01/2005 – I got my first job as a camera operator on Capitol Hill in Washington, DC, which I hated, and burned out quickly.

06/2005 – I left that job to start my first companies, RPN Photography, and (Insert Name Here) Productions. I took out $35,000 in credit card debt to finance this company.

09/2005 – I started production on my first short films, including *Going Home*, which eventually turned into *Connections*, my first web series.

2006

06/2006 – I closed my first company, (Insert Name Here) Productions, due to irreconcilable differences.

09/2006 – I flew to Denmark to help shoot a movie. I made barely anything on the production, but I got a $10,000 vacation out of it and had a good time for three weeks, so at least it was something. I ended up spending more preparing my gear than I made on the shoot in the end, though.

11/2006 – I don't remember the exact date, but at some time around here, my dad retired and ended up moving in with us for several months before he relocated to Pennsylvania with his wife. We were really struggling, and this helped. After he moved out, my best friend moved into our second bedroom so that we could afford our place, and he stayed there until we moved to California.

12/2006 – I started my first producer job as an executive producer for 100Dimensions, a nascent internet TV platform. I produced a TV pilot and commercial while there, including securing over 1,000 hours of content for the network. Even though this job paid well, we were in so much debt my dad kept living with us during his transition so we could stay above water.

2007

01/2007 – I started production on my first full-length movie, *Connections*. It wouldn't come out until 2013 and has currently made -$30,000, including literally $0 in revenue.

09/2007 – I directed a reality show pilot called *Sabers and Roses,* a show that went nowhere past a trailer, though I was paid for it, which was nice. The trailer looked okay, too.

2008

01/2008 – I got in a major car accident and lost my job because I couldn't work. I couldn't do anything for six months, so I started writing hardcore. This is still the only job I've ever had that paid me a regular salary for being a creative, aside from the ones I created for myself. This was when things started spiraling.

04/2008 – Closed RPN Photography since I couldn't use my gear anymore due to my injuries. I sold almost all my equipment, too.

06/2008 – Moved to Los Angeles at the beginning of the financial crisis. It was not the business, and there were no jobs at all. I ended up on unemployment for the full 99 weeks Obama-era recovery plan.

2009

02/2009 – I got my first manager, and he got me zero paid work over several years working with him.

2010

03/2010 – I directed the web series *Save Point,* which was never finished because the producer decided not to pay for compositing and abandoned it.

05/2010 – I don't remember the exact date, but we closed BNS Media Group around this time, as the movie was still not done, and we all moved on. It would take three more years for *Connections* to finally come out, and when it finally did, it wasn't long enough for a feature, so we cut it into a web series.

07/2010 – I brought my first comic to SDCC and was roundly rejected by every publisher and laughed at by some. I came back and vowed to make the kinds of books I wanted to make. I literally dropped thousands of dollars on this book, and we didn't have money, so it was really hard to hear that rejection.

09/2010 – At some point around here, my car accident settlement came in after years of negotiation and torching my relationship with my lawyer. I promptly used this money to fund two comics you might have heard of: *Ichabod Jones: Monster Hunter* and *Katrina Hates the Dead*. Without that settlement check, I would not be here today, as it kept me going for a couple of years.

11/2010 – I signed my first publishing deal for *Ichabod Jones: Monster Hunter* for $0. I never made $1 on this publishing contract.

2011

07/2011 – I did my first signing at SDCC, while launching my first (failed) Indiegogo campaign for *Katrina Hates Dead Shit* for $1340, the first real money I ever made on my own work.

2012

01/2012 – I launched my second (failed) Indiegogo campaign for *Katrina Hates Dead Shit* which made $145.

03/2012 – Ichabod was initially released by my first publisher. Again, I never made $1 on this book.

06/2012 – I signed my first novel publishing contract for Gumshoes for a $0 advance.

11/2012 – I signed my first option deal for $0.

2013

06/2013 – I had my *Ichabod* rights returned to me.

07/2013 – I had my first signing for *Katrina Hates the Dead* at SDCC as a trial for a publisher, and I sold out of all the books we brought. However, we didn't end up signing with that publisher.

2014

06/2014 – *Gumshoes* published. I still have made $0 on publishing.

09/2014 – *Ichabod Jones* Kickstarter launched. This was the LITERAL first success I ever had with a project after almost 10 years of trying. I made more on this launch than all the rest of my books combined.

10/2014 – I recovered rights to *Gumshoes* from the publisher and founded Wannabe Press. I had to pay a bunch of money to recover the rights to my books, but it was worth it.

2015

02/2015 – I released my first slate of books.

06/2015 – I left my job as a sales manager to pursue my company full-time. It was a very hard time, and I barely made it through the first year. I did not leave my job amicably, but I felt I had no choice but to quit, which put me in a tough financial place.

08/2015 – I signed my first option that PAID for *My Father Didn't Kill Himself*, which netted me a few thousand dollars, more than I made for the Kickstarter that I would run a few months later for that book.

09/2015 – I launched *Katrina Hates the Dead* on Kickstarter. This was my first "hit book", literally 10 years after graduating college and trying to make it as a creative. This book kept my company in business for two years by itself.

2016

01/2016 – I launched *My Father Didn't Kill Himself*, which, while successful, raised less than half of *Katrina*.

05/2016 – I launched the first and only book I published by another person, which scarred me so bad I vowed never to do it again. It raised barely half of *My Father Didn't Kill Himself*.

08/2016 – I launched *Spaceship Broken, Needs Repairs*, which made even less than my previous book.

11/2016 – Not only did my grandfather die, but our house was robbed, and they stole the last of my camera gear.

2017

02/2017 – I launched *Monsters and Other Scary Shit*, my first bonafide hit when I was 34. Up until this point, I was barely holding it together and barely able to keep the lights on. This was 16 years after graduating high school, 13 years after graduating college, and 12 years after starting to try to make a go of it.

09/2017 – I launched *Pixie Dust,* my second hit, cementing that I wasn't a one-hit-wonder. I had my first $100,000 year.

2018

09/2018 – I launched *Cthulhu is Hard to Spell,* my biggest title ever, which was delayed for three months from fulfillment by the first and only time I have used a fulfillment house.

2019

03/2019 – I launched the first Godsverse titles on Amazon/other platforms, and they went so badly that I became suicidal because I thought my career was completely over, and I had spent over $15,000 on making books that weren't selling.

09/2019 – Launched *Ichabod Jones: Monster Hunter* #5, trying to jumpstart something, and it raised over $16,000.

2020

01/2020 – I relaunched The Godvserse Chronicles on Kickstarter and recouped all my money, along with enough to pay for a fifth title.

03/2020 – I launched *Cthulhu is Hard to Spell: The Terrible Twos,* which raised over $30,000. Meanwhile, shows dried up, and I lost all revenue outside of Kickstarter.

06/2020 – I released my Summer Slate of books, which raised over $9,000, and repaid all my production costs.

09/2020 – I launched *Ichabod Jones* volume 2, and it raised over $20,000.

11/2020 – I released *How NOT to Invade Earth* and made over $3,000, paying off my production costs for this book I drew.

2021

01/2021 – I launched the second Godsverse Chronicles Kickstarter and broke through the $10,000 barrier.

03/2021 – I launched *Ichabod Jones* volume 3 and raised over $22,000.

04/2021 – I finished production on The Godsverse Chronicles, my first long series, which I started in June 2017.

These days, there are more ups than downs instead of more downs than ups. Some years a lot happened. In other years barely anything happened. Still, in other years mostly bad stuff happened, and I prayed for the days when nothing happened.

It looks like it's all good now, and in many ways, it is, but for the first nearly 15 years of my career, it was a lot of downs and very few ups. Still today, there are plenty of bad things happening I don't talk about – projects that stall, money wasted, launches that don't go as I planned – but there is enough good to wash that out and keep me moving forward.

I spent over $100,000 before I started to turn it around, and I figure I only broke even on all that money in 2017 after a lot of long-suffering years.

Still, for any of you struggling right now, know that you are not alone, and you can recover. There's still hope.

I'll be honest. I only made it here because my wife believed in me. I didn't believe myself most days. In fact, for the first decade of my career, there was incredible guilt as she carried me financially and emotionally.

It's only now that I don't feel that anymore, and the imposter syndrome has worn off. However, truth be told, I still feel like that some days.

5 STEPS TO WRITING FREEDOM

I've been thinking a lot about the mechanics of a successful writing career, and I've created a five-step process for how to think about the stages of a writing career if you want to make something that is sustainable for the long haul.

1. WRITE GREAT BOOKS

When you start, you suck at writing, so the first step is to get really good at making the thing you want to make. Practice and practice and practice every form of that craft, and try everything until you can confidently create work that resonates with people.

When people's eyes start going wide when you explain what you've made or when you show them what you've made, and you can repeat that feeling over and over, you are probably making something pretty great.

2. FIND YOUR "HIT"

Just because you know how to write a great book doesn't mean you know how to make a hit. A hit is something that breaks through and is financially profitable, and generates marketing without much effort.

While it's tempting to go with your first book as your "hit", every project has a natural ceiling that it can't get above.

It's likely your first book isn't a hit. You've never made money, so you think a little bit of money is a hit, which skews your perception.

Some books have a low ceiling, and others have a high ceiling. You need to find a project that resonates with your audience enough to generate exponential growth with every release, is easy to sell without much effort, and generates reliable income over the long term.

This is usually not your first book, which means you need to ping the water with several releases searching for the one people will resonate with quickly and easily, and talk about with other people, because word-of-mouth advertising is the most valuable form of advertising.

For me, that first hit was *Katrina Hates the Dead*. It sold on my table without much effort, allowing me to build my company and a reputation.

3. DOUBLE DOWN

Once you find your hit, it's time to double down and create a lot of work in that universe and plan multiple releases to test the viability and sustainability of your hit.

Hopefully, your hit will generate income over the long haul with reliability.

After Katrina, I made *Pixie Dust* in the same universe, and it raised $25,000 at launch, immediately becoming a hit. It was much easier to build upon a universe that was already successful than to build something from scratch.

4. PUSH

Push to move that hit into the lexicon until it can self-generate sales on its own and deliver reliable income.

This should allow you to stabilize marketing and production costs. The goal is to understand that if you spend X, you will get back Y reliably over time. Work this until the system self-stabilizes itself, and you know you can put $1 into the system and extract $2.

Once we had *Katrina Hates the Dead* and *Pixie Dust*, we could go to shows and know our costs and the expected ROI, allowing us to scale up. I've now written eleven books in the Godsverse Chronicles, with 11 planned, and an additional graphic novel.

5. FINANCE THE FUTURE

Once that hit has broken through and delivers reliable income every month and every launch, use the funds to finance other potential hits.

This is where we added *Cthulhu is Hard to Spell,* an even bigger hit than The Godsverse Chronicles, and were able to drop enough money to turn *Ichabod Jones: Monster Hunter* into a hit, too.

Now, I have several "hits". The Godsverse Chronicles, *Cthulhu is Hard to Spell,* and *Ichabod Jones: Monster Hunter.*

If you can find four reliable hits that you can release once a year, you have a sustainable creative business making the thing you love, and you'll never have to worry about when the next payday will come.

As you grow, you'll also begin to develop a backlist of profitable and saleable properties that can be combined into powerful bundles that can grow your income over time.

BE YOU

I have been in a heated spat with somebody over email who thinks my welcome email turns people off. I have been trying to impart to her that the point is to make the wrong people run away and to drive the right people to my brand and to engage with me.

It didn't work to turn her around, of course, because she wasn't the right human to hear my message. My emails were made to drive her away because she isn't a good fit for my message.

I tried to educate her nonetheless, though, because it's an important concept that most people will never understand.

They think everybody needs to love them, but the truth is that no matter what you do, most people will dislike or 'nothing' you.

Most potential customers won't even dislike you. Most people will 'nothing' you. They won't care about anything you say, even if you scream at them. If you are bland and homogeneous, trying to cater to everybody, your message will be so watered down nobody will respond to it.

And if nobody responds to it, you are dead in the water. There is so much sensory information out there trying to grab people's attention, you have to plant your flag and make sure that people know why they should care.

Then, there is another truth that will rear its ugly head if you try to please everyone.

You can't.

No matter what you do, some people are going to hate it. If you're polite, they will call you too nice. If you're whimsical, they will call you weird. If you are helpful, they will call you fake.

If you worry about pleasing everyone, you will worry too much about those who hate you, and there will be people who hate you. The more success you have, the more people will hate you. You can't focus on them, or you will drown.

You have to focus on the people who love you and your work and cater everything to them. There's no other way to survive in this world.

If you want to find those people, you have to be yourself 110%. You have to call out to those people to find you. If you instead water down your message, you might as well not even try because nobody will hear it, and you won't find the people who love your work.

And that would be a travesty.

GOOD ADVICE

The best advice is usually the most boring.

It doesn't get a lot of shares. It doesn't have a ton of likes. It doesn't go viral. People don't gossip about it on every social media channel.

There aren't many influencers peddling good advice because it doesn't get attention, and that is what influencers crave.

Attention is fleeting, so loud advice overtakes good advice.

Good advice sits there, like a rock, waiting to be found, waiting for people to turn it over, and completely content never to be found. There's no need to guard good advice because almost nobody wants it, and when they hear it, they ignore it because good advice doesn't demand to be heard.

People who give good advice are quite happy to let their success speak for itself, so they don't spend much time hammering it into people.

They are too busy doing it.

Almost every piece of advice I hear is garbage, but it's loud, so I know people will listen.

And because it's loud and easy to consume, it spreads like a virus.

Then people follow that advice to their doom because following easy advice is easy.

Following good advice is hard.

Good advice tends to be expensive, too. Expensive to learn, expensive to implement, at least in time, and expensive to validate.

Sometimes it takes years and years of work to mold good advice into something that works, but when you do, good advice is eternal.

And things that take years aren't sexy. They are just right because they have stood the test of time.

I have watched the greatest minds of my generation spoiled by bad advice.

Meanwhile, good advice endures, not because of virality, but because it works.

It carries on because the flame is nurtured, and when somebody else succeeds with it, they become the standard-bearer. They make sure the fire doesn't go out.

Any loud advice you receive is probably bad advice. Good advice is whispered for fear that the candle will go out if you speak too loudly and for respect to all the standard-bearers who came before.

It's readily available, though. You just have to look for it and find people that peddle in it.

They are probably not going to be flashy...because they let their success speak for them.

DISAPPOINTMENT

I'm going to let you in on a little secret about how I come up with some of my best ideas.

Have you ever read a book, taken a course, or bought a product only to be disappointed?

Has it ever happened to you again and again?

Me too.

In fact, a big part of my business starts with disappointment. It's trying a lot of products or courses and never finding anything that was...well, that was ever very good. I always enter a new market with the best intentions to use the products that already exist. However, more often than not, I sample all the products, and none get them right.

They might have a piece of the puzzle, maybe, but nobody has the complete picture. Some of them might miss the mark completely. So, a lot of my work comes from one simple question:

"What would it look like if this was done well?"

Most things, even the worst things, have a spark of genius, which, if harnessed properly, can improve your existing products.

ECOSYSTEM

An ecosystem is fragile. Introduce the wrong animals or vegetation, and it could send a perfectly balanced system into chaos.

Conversely, removing the wrong animals or vegetation could do the same.

The same is true with any industry or even in your own practice.

Too often, people take on every responsibility thrown at them, whether it's ideas for books, potential partnerships, conventions, or marketing efforts, without any thought as to how it will affect their ecosystem.

Part of this is naivete.

At the beginning of your career, you don't know how your ecosystem works. You also don't have the opportunity to turn down much work without setting yourself back.

So, you take on more and more.

Then, you establish yourself but never take the time to figure out how your ecosystem works. So you continue throwing junk and trash into your ecosystem until it is on the verge of destruction, leading to burnout or worse.

To find equilibrium with yourself, you have to find a balance that is right for you, jettisoning things that don't serve you, doubling down on things that light you up, and having enough space to recover.

The same is true when trying to place yourself in an industry. Whether it's comics, book publishing, magazines, or the world of food trucks, you need to find a way to become a beneficial part of the ecosystem...

...because if you aren't, the ecosystem will treat you as a cancerous growth to protect itself against.

I'm not saying be compliant. I am definitely not compliant. It does mean finding out how your message and your work can work inside the ecosystem.

If you're thinking of a series you're writing, for instance, a good exercise is placing your series against the other big hitters in your genre and trying to find out how it can complement the other books while bringing a new perspective.

Too often, authors are quick to put down the other books in their genre, but while that gets good "engagement," it is not "good engagement," and people quickly tire of it.

It behooves you to find out how your book complements the rest of the books in your genre but fills a hole that your readers can connect with easily.

Katrina Hates the Dead, the book that seeded my career, was a satire on post-apoc books with my own little fantasy spin thrown in there.

When I pitched it, I always talked about how much I loved those books, and still do, but I found the fact that they all started the day after the Apocalypse tiring after a while, and I wanted to tell a story that started years after the Apocalypse when it became rote.

There are more stories like that now, but back in 2015, there weren't very many, so it complemented the overall landscape in a new and interesting way while still holding reverence to the genre as a whole.

When Monica Leonelle convinced me to come back to non-fiction, I decided this time I would not be a burr in the heel of the industry, telling it everything it was doing wrong.

Instead, I would show how the processes I used complemented those that already existed and made up for deficiencies that everyone knew existed to make the whole ecosystem work better.

Authors work in secret for a lot of their lives, and even though we have support from other authors/publishers, we don't often think about the ecosystem as a whole and how we operate inside of it.

Whenever I take on a project, I try to think about how the series, the engagement, or the course, will help build ecosystems; the industry's, the genre's, and my own.

EXPERT

People often ask me about non-fiction and how to become an expert in a subject that people quote and seek out.

This is a heavy question for me because I don't think this about myself, but I do have an answer from my own life, and I think in the past year, it's borne out in the success of the Kickstarter book + Accelerator.

It's a pretty simple philosophy that I've cultivated since I started teaching back in 2010:

Live in the community you want to serve, stake out a position that is underserved or unknown and complementary to the industry at large, and then keep having success with that position until you're so successful people have to take notice.

The main problem with most people trying to be an "expert" is that they trash the industry they are in and the thought leaders currently doing the work.

I have been that person in the past, but in all honesty, you need those experts to validate you to the audience at large.

I've been screaming about Kickstarter for almost a decade, but it wasn't until I started playing the game a bit better when an expert took me under her wing and told others to pay attention that they began to do so.

And the reason she did was because I kept having success in this weird thing called Kickstarter that few people were talking about except for me and DWS.

And the way we broke through the noise was by showing people how it could complement their existing systems and revolutionize them.

So many "experts" want to blow up the game, but the game has been working for a long time, and there is simply too much inertia to break people from it completely.

The truth is people ARE having success with every strategy out there right now, but it's not working for everyone, and those people are the ones you can help, along with those very successful authors who want to have even more success.

Instead of trashing everything, stake out a position that is underutilized or antithetical to what other people are doing, and prove that it can COMPLEMENT their current process, not destroy it completely.

Kickstarter is something you can put at the front end of ANY launch and add hundreds or thousands of dollars that can be injected straight into your retailer launch.

The retailer launch, AMS ads, Facebook ads, etc., is a process people already know, and the problem with most launches is that authors often don't have the capital to properly promote them.

Kickstarter completely revolutionizes that ONE problem and complements the rest of a book launch in a natural way.

It solves a MASSIVE problem in the publishing community, and I happened to have had success in it for long enough that I had a system to share, and Monica Leonelle knew how to bring that to authors in a way that made sense to them.

If we came up with a brand new system that made people blow up everything and start from scratch, we would have met with lots of friction, not just from authors but from the established providers already making money from how the system works.

Monica and I lived in the publishing community for over a decade each, so we knew how to position it. The younger me did not know how to position it.

Now I do.

If you're having problems with breaking through, one or more of the following is true.

- You haven't done it long enough.
- You haven't had enough success with it.
- You don't live in the community you want to serve.
- You don't know how to position your offer.
- Your offer isn't something people want.
- You are trying to be a thorn in the side of the industry instead of a complement to it, alienating the people who need to hype your system.

I've been a thorn before, and it got me nowhere. I've had every one of the problems listed above, and it wasn't until I found alignment with them that I started to have success.

LEAD

The synthesis of 10 years of first-hand experience building a creative business comes down to one sentence:

Everybody wants to be a part of things, but nobody wants to put them together.

This has been true with publishing, anthologies, podcasts, blogs, conventions, and with literally everything I've done.

If you can take it on the chin and do the work of organizing things, then people will follow you, especially when you prove your things are good.

This is inclusive of fandoms, too. Everybody wants to be a part of fun fandoms, but they don't want to do the work of leading them.

Yes, you have to make the thing great, but once you have a proven model, people will fall in line...

...it's the one truth I have learned.

People love being organized, but they hate organizing. They love learning helpful information, but they hate gathering it. They love curated content, but they hate curating it.

They want all the rewards with none of the work, so if you can do the work of finding them, gathering them, and continuing to engage them, you will win.

ABJECT FAILURE

Here is the problem with calling any project a failure.

There are so many points of failure that cause a project to seem like a failure, but it doesn't mean the project itself is a failure.

Let us take a book, for example. Yes, it is possible that the book is horrible. However, if you are running an ad for a book, there are so many pieces that could lead to failure, even if the book is great. For instance:

On the ad level:

- The ad copy might not be right.
- The targeting could not be right.
- You could be targeting the wrong audience.
- You could have launched at the wrong time of day.
- You could have launched on the wrong day of the week.
- You could be targeting the right audience, but your ad isn't being served to the right people.
- The audience you chose might not be big enough.
- The imagery you are using might be wrong.
- The competition for ads might be higher than normal.

- A more popular book might be going after the same audience.

Additionally:

- Ad costs might be higher because of the time of year, like at Christmastime when companies blow their remaining ad budget for the year.
- People might be away from their computers more because it is summer and they are with their families.
- A world event might be diverting attention from your advertisements.

And if you can get a great ad that gets people to click, the fun doesn't stop there:

- The copy on your page might not be strong enough.
- Your tagline might not be compelling.
- Your cover image might be weak.
- Your cover image might not be aimed at the right market.
- Your blurb might be aimed at the wrong market.

And then, even if you can get somebody to read your book:

- Maybe the first page isn't amazing, and they put it down, even though the rest of the book is great.
- Maybe the book isn't written to market.
- Maybe you have written a book into an oversaturated market.
- Maybe trends have shifted.
- Maybe you haven't created good enough hooks at the end of each chapter.
- Maybe you haven't written a series.

And that's just SOME of the things that could happen with a single type of project that might prevent it from being successful, and if all of those things go PERFECTLY, then maybe you will have a hit, but maybe you won't because some other thing I didn't list went wrong.

The good news is that you can tweak any and all of these things and relaunch your book, or any product, again and again until it's right and you find the perfect audience for it. Most projects aren't failures. It's the marketing that is a failure.

But even if your project is an abject failure, that does not make you a failure.

SURVIVORSHIP BIAS

People always quote survivors.

The Lindsay Burokers, the Mark Dawsons, the Linsey Halls, the Amanda Hockings, but for every one of those, there are a thousand that came out at the same time, did everything right, and never caught fire, or burned brightly for a second and then flamed out.

Yes, thousands of authors make a living self-publishing, but millions more struggle to make it worthwhile, and tens of millions more have tried and failed.

Acknowledging only the survivors does a disservice to your career and distorts the truth about being a successful author, which is more than just having a great cover, a killer blurb, and a great story.

Way too much of it is just dumb luck, and way too much of what's left is just pushing forward to the bitter end, way past the point other people, any sane person, would give up to push through the other side.

Tacking your north star to a successful author is fine and well, but don't ignore the fact that the sea is littered with the bodies of authors past.

LAUNCH ALREADY

I'm a planner—quite a planner, actually, especially when it comes to launching products.

I tend to launch big projects, and only when the entire project is complete. I am all for waiting until the timing is right and you can maximize your potential. But, on the other hand, sometimes you just have to launch the thing and see how it does.

Eventually, once everything is checked and double-checked, all you can do is launch the thing and hope for the best. After all, eventually, there's nothing else you can do to prepare. Eventually, you've run out of checks, and it's time to send it off into the world.

Here's the cruel twist of fate.

No matter how much you prepare, it's probably not going to go as well as you expect...at least not at first. So especially for your first projects, just get them out there. There are no expectations. If they suck...nobody will even notice. If they are great... nobody will probably notice. Sure, you always want the maximum number of people to be exposed to your brand, but honestly, you're waiting too long to launch.

Listen to me, as a friend, and really hear my words.

Just launch it already. You've waited long enough. We're sick of hearing about it. We want to see it already. Just do the thing already. If the launch sucks, then just relaunch it, and if that one sucks, just relaunch it again.

Or launch the next thing. But you gotta launch it already so you can do better next time.

NO SINGLE THING

Being somebody who has failed does not make you a failure, even if all you have known is being unsuccessful.

Not having found love yet does not mean you are unloveable, even if you have never known love.

Screwing up does not mean you are a screw-up, even if you never seem to get it right.

Current states can be changed and often change quickly and without warning.

You are not one thing. You are many things and have the potential to be anything.

FUNDING MECHANICS

Possibly the most important question to answer when moving into a creative career is this:

What is your funding mechanic for project creation?

For most creative types, their full-time job is their funding mechanic, at least at first. They use their paycheck to funnel money into their projects, which may or may not be financially successful on their own.

For many full-time creatives, freelance work is the funding mechanic they use for project creation. They use the money earned from their freelance work to fund the creation of other projects.

For some creatives, their projects are "self-funded", meaning they generate enough revenue to be profitable, or at least revenue-neutral, without needing any other income to fund them.

Still, other creators have one or two projects that are SO SUCCESSFUL that they fund everything else.

For a long time, I was in the first group. Then the second, the third, and finally, the fourth.

I'm very lucky that almost all my projects are self-funded eventually, but that usually takes 1-2 years, at least, before

I can see returns on them. Until they can self-fund, I still need capital from my uber-successful books to pay for the start-up costs of a new series.

Generally, I am spinning up at least one series at all times that hasn't been launched yet.

For years I used the profits from Ichabod, the Godsverse Chronicles, and *Cthulhu is Hard to Spell* to not only fund those projects but also funnel money into other projects that haven't launched yet.

When a creator struggles, it's often a failure to properly realize the answer to their funding mechanic. There are no right or wrong answers to this question, but it is a question that needs to be answered so that you know how to build your business.

SKUNKS

We have a family of three skunks living under our porch. This is not the first year a skunk has taken purchase under our porch, but usually, they only stay a couple of days, and then they are gone to the next house.

This family has been there for weeks, and they smell terrible.

Now, I am usually pretty tolerant of the natural species living around me. I know we are an invasive species and the skunks were here before me.

However, last night it came to a head. I woke up at 2 am, the smell so noxious it made my stomach turn, and I couldn't sleep.

So, this morning I set out to find a solution. I called about thirty places, talked to a dozen, and had three come out for a quote.

Most of them didn't even bother to pick up the phone.

Now, the twist…we're leaving on Monday for two weeks, so this needed to be fixed ASAP. I did not want to come home to this smell or worse, and I didn't have time for a "maybe" solution.

The first two said the same things. They would place traps and then come every day to check. They cannot guarantee anything, and it would cost somewhere from $200-$800, and they wouldn't do anything about the horrible smell.

Then the third person came, and he was super personable. Not that the first two weren't cordial, but this one played with the dogs and spent a ton of time going through the whole house.

When he was done, he told me it would cost about $4,500, somewhere between 5x-40x the other quotes.

And I said, "heck yes".

Why? Because they told me:

- I would never have to deal with this again.
- They would dissipate the smell.
- They would prevent other animals from using pheromones as a homing beacon to our house.
- That they would fix everything, so I wouldn't have to worry about it.

…and they told me they would fix it TOMORROW.

It was everything I wanted, and while $4500 was a lot to take, this wasn't the first time this problem had happened. It's been a habitual problem.

So, I paid the deposit, and I was happy to do it.

There is a lesson in all this.

Almost every one of us competes on price, and while price is important (I always shop around), what matters most is value and how you can ease a person's pain.

If their pain point is high and your value is high, then the price doesn't matter nearly as much. If you make the best product, then you can charge more for it.

This is easier to see in non-fiction, but it is also true in fiction.

One of the main pain points in fiction is finding new books that resonate with a reader. Once a reader finds your books and falls in love, one of the main pain points you are relieving in them is that they don't have to look for another writer while they make their way through your catalog.

We don't talk about this pain point much, but that doesn't mean it's not there. It can take hundreds of reading hours to find something that resonates, and that connection is precious.

As somebody that reads over 100 books a year, I will tell you that there is no greater relief than connecting with an author's work and seeing they have a slew of other books I can dig my way through for a while.

This is enough to justify premium pricing in and of itself, and people will pay top dollar not to have to search for another author for months.

I will, at least, and I'm not some special snowflake, so there must be many other people like me.

And there are.

I know there are others like me because I see them back my books when I launch books for a premium price on Kickstarter, and I see it when our students launch books on Kickstarter, too.

People are willing to pay top dollar for books from their favorite authors because there is a high likelihood that they will love them.

That's worth a lot.

It's why people voraciously dig into series, because there is something that resonates with them, and it doesn't come along often.

I would pay so much money never to have to read a book that doesn't resonate with me again for the rest of my life.

ANTHOLOGIES

I have done a lot of anthologies, and here is my quick and dirty theory on running them

They are hard. They are complicated. They are pains in the butt, and you will make no money on them.

Even my best-selling anthologies barely made me any money.

The most important reason to put together an anthology, aside from working with some of the most amazing creators in the world, is if you are making an anthology that will funnel into your other work.

It is a singularly amazing tool for that, maybe the best tool in your toolkit, as it can actually make you money while being a valuable marketing asset.

Your anthology is the best shot you have of bringing in a bunch of like-minded people into the rest of your work.

The first *Monsters and Other Scary Shit* book raised $27,000 on Kickstarter, and its purpose was to bring awareness from the right fans to then buy *Pixie Dust*, which ended up raising $25,000 at launch, and those two books launched everything else.

That first anthology funneled into the *Pixie Dust* book and directly launched my career into the next level, just like Cthulhu funnels directly into Ichabod.

Putting together an anthology is a labor of love and pain. If you aren't using it as a lead magnet for the rest of your work, then you are going to waste all that effort because an anthology is a grueling process.

Don't make a "Cthulhu" anthology just because it's hot. Find something exciting for YOUR NICHE READER, the kind that will read ALL your other work, and make THAT anthology.

It's the only way an anthology makes sense.

SET PIECES

With the *Oscars* last night, I have been thinking a lot about set pieces for the past few days.

No, I'm not talking about production design. I'm talking about the big, epic moments that a movie is built around and anchors the plot.

Every TV season or movie has a couple of big, blow-out moments that they build to for the majority of the runtime.

Every moment can't be a huge set piece because they take up a huge amount of the budget. They must be used judiciously.

For instance, the end of *Avengers: Endgame*, the big battle between Thanos and the Avengers, is a set piece.

They will generally happen at the end of a movie during the climax, in the middle to end of the second act, and 1-2 other times during the movie, depending on the run time.

Every single movie has this construction. Set pieces are where most of the "best" trailer moments come from and often distill the plot to its essence.

The rest of the movie is really building up to these huge moments of catharsis.

For this year's Oscar-winning movie, *Parasite*, there were three "set pieces" basically set up at the end of the first act, the end of the second act, and the third act.

For TV shows, they might only get one big set piece every three episodes.

There's a great episode of *Community* that happens right after an episode where there's a big, epic paintball battle where they are all stuck in a room trying to decide who stole Annie's pen.

And Abed shouts out, "It's a bottle episode!"

A bottle episode is one where all the characters are stuck in one place, and this tends to happen because the producers blew their budget on a HUGE set piece in a previous episode and now need to conserve their budget by shooting something cheaply.

The set pieces destroy the old paradigm, release tension from the previous scenes, and move the story in a new direction.

The rest of the show is simply moving the pieces around the board to build up to these set pieces.

For movies, the budgetary reasons are clear, but the story reasons resonate in any story, even if it's a book or comic.

The story reason for set pieces is that when everything is explosions and car chases, the audience gets bored. It's like listening to an entire album where the music is super fast.

It becomes hard to remember any single song because they all sound the same. The best stories have an ebb and flow to them.

They build and then release tension. They show character growth and let the audience acclimate to the new normal.

However, the audience also needs direction to know where to focus their attention, which is how set pieces work as a waypoint for them.

In a romance book, these might be the "meet-cute", the "first date", the "break-up", and the "get back together".

In a mystery, it might be "the first look at the crime scene", "the big clue", "the wrongful accusation", and the "true culprit".

You only get so many set pieces in a book because the audience needs time to recover and adjust from the previous set piece.

This makes your job as a writer a bit easier because when constructing a plot, you only need to FOR SURE know your set piece moments.

The end is easy to imagine because it's your biggest set piece, but if you work back and set up another set piece every 10,000-20,000 words of a book, then the rest of your decisions are just about moving the piece on the board to get to that set piece.

It's a great way for "pantsers" to put a little plotting into their books to make sure they don't get lost.

You're allowed, then, to meander around and do whatever you want, as long as you're moving toward the next set piece.

The build-up to the set piece gets more rapid as you approach it, and the stakes rise with every passing page.

Then, after the set piece, there is a cooling-off period where the character and audience acclimate to the new normal, regroup, and figure out what to do next.

Then, the tension builds to another set piece, culminating with a catharsis of tension, and you repeat the process through the story.

The book becomes all about tightening the tension and releasing it. When you think of your story that way, it becomes easy to see if something is serving the plot or needs to be cut.

Depending on the length of a story, you might only have one set piece. For instance, in a comic book, you are probably going to get at most TWO set pieces per issue, right in the middle and then at the end.

The rest is all building up and releasing tension, and strengthening the bond between the audience and the character.

UNTIL

Nobody wants you until...

...until you start making money.

...until you have an audience.

...until you start booking appearances.

...until people start talking about you.

...until you don't need them.

...until you speak so loudly they can't deny you.

...until you cause a ruckus so big they can't turn away.

...until everybody's talking about you wherever they turn.

Nobody wants you until you show them you can print money for them, and then it's too late...

...because then you can print money for yourself.

Then, you can call your own shots.

CREATING AND MARKETING

Most creators I know have lamented to me at least once about how they want to create and not have to worry about marketing. Since I'm trying to meet you where you are, I'll give you a couple of my favorite ways you can market AND create at the same time.

Be a part of anthology projects - apply for anthology projects, and when you're accepted, you automatically have an in with the editor, the other creators, and anybody who reads the book. It's a perfect way to expand your network AND audience while creating. A good benchmark is 5-6 anthology projects a year. While you won't make much money, you will be creating while doing marketing.

Editing anthology projects - editing IS creating, so editing an anthology and being the one who puts it together is creating while you market, as you'll have your name front and center for every person who hears about, checks out, or works on the project.

Do guest posts/pin-ups for other creators - if you have an audience LIKE another person, then you can do creating while you market by offering to do pieces for them, either a short story or a pin-up, or even a guest comic. You'll be getting in front of other people's audiences AND creating new things.

Drawing/writing fanart - plenty of well-known artists got their start doing fan art and writing stories in other universes. Ones you would recognize, and you can leverage yourself by having a distinctive voice in a genre you are passionate about creating in while you are creating and marketing yourself. If it's popular, you can even repurpose it like E L James did with *Fifty Shades of Grey.*

Write magazine articles or draw for newspaper magazines that service your ideal readers - there are always media outlets that need new editorial cartoons, reviewers, and other creatives.

Do a crossover project with all of your characters - this is tried and true in comics, in art, and to some degree, even in novels. Each person works on a part of the story or the piece of art, and together you bring all your fans to it and promote it together. This is like an anthology, but you aren't making different pieces, you are making one piece that has all your footprints on it.

Volunteer for an organization you care about doing art or stories - many organizations have big networks that can help elevate your work.

Do live streams with other artists/writers where you create a jam piece or do your own work while you're on their stream - you can make a piece for you to sell after the live stream while you are working on it for either your audience or whoever's stream you are on at the time, literally creating while you market.

Those are some of my best thoughts about how to market WHILE you create.

TERMS

It's time to come to terms with what you've done in your career up until this point.

I talk to a lot of creators, and the weight most of them carry around their necks is "I wish I had done more", or "I wish I had done that", or "I wish I hadn't done that".

Here's the hard truth:

You can't do anything about your career up until yesterday. You've already written those books. You've already wasted that time. You've already lost that publishing contract. You've already spilled your energy into one thing or another.

However, that is not wasted time, either. It was a time in which you learned things, and you can use that to twist the future to your advantage.

I know because it happened to me, too.

I love Ichabod, I really do, but for years people used it to label me as a horror author when I am, in fact, a fantasy author.

I have nothing against horror authors, but if you come into my work expecting horror, you will be sorely disappointed.

I use none of the conventions of horror storytelling in my stories.

I take horror elements and use them to tell fantasy stories.

Yes, if you are open-minded about the types of horror you consume, I think you will absolutely love my books, but I am not Stephen King. I'm much more like Terry Pratchett or Michael Moorcock than anyone else.

People did the same thing with *Katrina Hates the Dead.*

While it uses horror elements, it's a fantasy story with magic, gods, and all the conventions of fantasy. If you expect horror when you read it, well, I still think you're going to have a good time, but it's not the book you think you'll get.

I also wrote a lot of "off-brand" not fantasy in my life, which meant when I really looked at my career, and the kind of thing I wanted to be known for, I had a couple of non-fiction books, some YA mystery, some sci-fi, and not a whole lot of fantasy.

It was depressing, honestly, when I sat down in 2016 to figure this all out and where I wanted to go with my career.

You might say, "why do I have to do one thing?", and it's because people will put you in a box. They will. I hate it, but they will, and when they put you in that box, you are expected to stay in that box.

Yes, you can step out of that box, but it's basically like starting your career all over again when you do. Some people will follow you between genres and formats, but most won't, and unless you have a huge audience, it's really hard to have enough of them willing to read your other stuff to make it profitable.

I'm all about creating what you want to create at the beginning of your career before you know what you want to do, and it took me a LONG time to figure out what kind of author I wanted to be.

In fact, I railed against the "people will know you as one thing" for a LONG time, and it wasn't until I released a bunch of off-brand stuff to crickets that I realized the truth of it all.

If you are going to step out of your box, you had better be willing to start your career all over again. I feel strongly about being a novelist. So strongly, in fact, that I was willing to go back to the beginning and build from scratch to make it work.

If you're aching to tell a story, then tell it, but know it probably won't catch unless you are willing to devote tons of resources to it. That doesn't make it any less important. Some of the most important things in life aren't financially lucrative.

So, back in 2016, I was branded as a horror author, but I really wrote fantasy. I had to come to terms with that idea first and then figure out how to turn it around.

It wasn't easy. I had a lot of sleepless nights where I kicked myself for all the "mistakes" I made in my career and all the projects I didn't make.

Eventually, I got over myself and decided I could still turn it around, even if it took a long time.

I did that by taking Ichabod and Katrina and turning them into the series they should have been all along.

Ichabod became a dark fantasy series with the introduction of Necromonica specifically and magic in general.

The truth was that I always intended Ichabod to be a fantasy story.

The first four issues just took some time to get there. When I brought Ichabod back in 2019, I made sure people saw it as a fantasy series right off the bat.

Then, with Katrina, I expanded the universe, now called The Godsverse Chronicles, which is super fantasy-y, made more fantasy comics with *Pixie Dust* and *Black Market Heroine*, and then I wrote a bunch more books in that universe that all highlight different aspects of fantasy, from dark to science, and everything in between.

I would be hard-pressed to find somebody who has read either series and still thinks they are horror books.

Plus, it has informed ALL my work since then. All my anthology pieces are fantasy. Even my own anthology series, *Cthulhu is Hard to Spell,* is about the mythology of Lovecraft's work.

I was able to take a career that was moving in a direction I didn't want and turn it back toward the direction I wanted it to go, all by coming to terms with where I was and where I wanted to go.

Ichabod and Katrina made my career. I love them, and fans, so much for taking a chance on them. They were a huge part of my ecosystem, and I simply couldn't imagine them not being a centerpiece of my career when it was all over.

But I had to do something to make sure I controlled the narrative and positioning of my career.

It's never too late until you are dead. I did this when I was 35, thinking my career was over, but it was just beginning. Whether you're younger or older than that, it's not too late for you either.

But you have to come to terms with the career, or lack of career, you have had until this point.

THE END?

Well, no. This is not the end because Facebook still exists…I assume, at least. I'm writing this in the past, after all.

Even if it doesn't, I still exist, and I will keep having thoughts about this being a writer and living a creative life as long as I still exist.

Some of those thoughts might even be relevant to you. Who knows? If you liked this book, you can find more over at kickstartyournovel.com, writermba.com, or russellnohelty.com.

If you did not like this collection of words, then I have both good and bad news.

The good news is that this particular collection of words is complete. I am honestly surprised you got to the end if you didn't like it, but at least it's over, yeah?

The bad news is that the collection of cells that wrote these words likely continues to exist and has probably written many more musings since it finished this book.

Good news, again…you don't have to read them. So, kind of a rollercoaster in the end.

And who knows? Maybe I will be irrelevant by the time you read this. Although, even when I was more irrelevant than I am now, I was still writing.

Long story short, if you liked it, find me online. If you didn't, then you probably shouldn't, but you still can if you want to.

Find more of my work at my blog:

www.theauthorstack.com

Find all my work at my website:

www.russellnohelty.com

Bookbub:

https://www.bookbub.com/profile/russell-nohelty

www.ingramcontent.com/pod-product-compliance
Lightning Source LLC
Chambersburg PA
CBHW071540210326
41597CB00019B/3064